ANIMAL FARM

PASTORALISM AND POLITICS

Richard I. Smyer

TWAYNE PUBLISHERS
An Imprint of Simon & Schuster Macmillan
NEW YORK

Prentice Hall International
LONDON   MEXICO CITY   NEW DELHI   SINGAPORE
SYDNEY   TORONTO

TWAYNE'S MASTERWORK STUDIES
ROBERT LECKER, GENERAL EDITOR

THE BIBLE: A LITERARY STUDY by *John H. Gottcent*
THE BIRTH OF TRAGEDY: A COMMENTARY by *David Lenson*
THE CANTERBURY TALES: A LITERARY PILGRIMAGE by *David Williams*
GREAT EXPECTATIONS: A NOVEL OF FRIENDSHIP by *Bert G. Hornback*
HEART OF DARKNESS: SEARCH FOR THE UNCONSCIOUS by *Gary Adelman*
THE INTERPRETATION OF DREAMS:
   FREUD'S THEORIES REVISITED by *Laurence M. Porter*
INVISIBLE MAN: RACE AND IDENTITY by *Kerry McSweeney*
JANE EYRE: PORTRAIT OF A LIFE by *Maggie Berg*
MIDDLEMARCH: A NOVEL OF REFORM by *Bert G. Hornback*
MOBY-DICK: ISHMAEL'S MIGHTY BOOK by *Kerry McSweeney*
PARADISE LOST: IDEAL AND TRAGIC EPIC by *Francis C. Blessington*
THE RED BADGE OF COURAGE: REDEFINING THE HERO by *Donald B. Gibson*
THE SCARLET LETTER: A READING by *Nina Baym*
SONS AND LOVERS: A NOVEL OF DIVISION AND DESIRE by *Ross C Murfin*
THE SUN ALSO RISES: A NOVEL OF THE TWENTIES by *Michael S. Reynolds*
TO THE LIGHTHOUSE: THE MARRIAGE OF LIFE AND ART by *Alice van Buren Kelley*
THE WASTE LAND: A POEM OF MEMORY AND DESIRE by *Nancy K. Gish*

ANIMAL FARM

PASTORALISM AND POLITICS

Richard I. Smyer

TWAYNE PUBLISHERS
BOSTON

A Division of G.K. Hall & Co.

Animal Farm: Pastoralism and Politics
Richard I. Smyer

Twayne's Masterworks Studies No. 19

Copyright 1988 by G.K. Hall & Co.
All rights reserved.
Twayne Publishers
An Imprint of Simon & Schuster Macmillan
866 Third Avenue
New York, NY 10022

Copyediting supervised by Barbara Sutton
Book production by Gabrielle B. McDonald

Typeset in 10/14 Sabon
by Compset, Inc., Beverly, Massachusetts

Printed on permanent/durable acid-free paper
and bound in the United States of America

Library of Congress Cataloging in Publication Data

Smyer, Richard I., 1935 —
   Animal farm : pastoralism and politics / Richard I. Smyer.
      p.   cm. — (Twayne's masterwork studies ; no. 19)
   Bibliography: p.
   Includes index.
   ISBN 0-8057-7980-9 (alk. paper).   ISBN 0-8057-8030-0 (pbk. : alk.
paper)
      1. Orwell, George, 1903-1950. Animal farm.   2. Pastoral fiction,
English—History and criticism.   3. Political fiction, English—
History and criticism.   I. Title.   II. Series
PR6029.R8A77 1988
823'.914—dc19   88-2974
                                                                            CIP

To Ernest Tilford for his dedicated service to Amnesty International and the general cause of human rights

CONTENTS

NOTE ON REFERENCES AND ACKNOWLEDGMENTS

CHRONOLOGY: GEORGE ORWELL'S LIFE AND WORKS

1. Historical Context   1
2. The Importance of the Work   7
3. Critical Reception   11

A READING

4. Introduction   23
5. Some *Per*versions of Pastoral   30
6. "That Infernal Palaeolithic Skull"   67
7. Trees into Books, Books into Trees   96

                               NOTES   135

               SELECTED BIBLIOGRAPHY   145

                               INDEX   149

                   ABOUT THE AUTHOR   154

NOTE ON REFERENCES AND ACKNOWLEDGMENTS

The edition of *Animal Farm* used in this study is the easily available Harcourt Brace 1946 edition. This author is obligated to Harcourt Brace Jovanovich and to A. M. Heath Ltd on behalf of the estate of the late Sonia Brownell Orwell and Martin Secker and Warburg Ltd (British Commonwealth rights) for permission to quote extracts from the following published and unpublished works by George Orwell: *Animal Farm, Burmese Days, A Clergyman's Daughter, The Collected Essays, Journalism and Letters, Coming Up For Air, Down and Out in Paris and London, Homage to Catalonia, Keep the Aspidistra Flying, Nineteen Eighty-Four, The Road to Wigan Pier,* and literary notebooks 1 and 3.

I am obligated to Denis Collings for permission to use the photograph from the Orwell Archive, University College, London, entitled "Eric Blair in Wallington Churchyard, 1939." I am grateful to Janet Percival and her staff at the University College Manuscript Reading Room for making available material from the Orwell Archive, and I am equally grateful to Jeanne Voyles and the staff of the interlibrary loan service of the University of Arizona. I wish to thank my typist, Beverly Cook, for a consistently professional level of work.

Excerpts from *Animal Farm* by George Orwell, copyright 1946 by Harcourt Brace Jovanovich, Inc.; renewed 1974 by Sonia Brownell Orwell. Reprinted by permission of the publisher.

Excerpts from *Burmese Days,* copyright 1934 by George Orwell;

Note On References and Acknowledgments

renewed 1962 by Sonia Pitt-Rivers. Reprinted by permission of Harcourt Brace Jovanovich, Inc.

Excerpts from *A Clergyman's Daughter, Coming Up for Air, Keep the Aspidistra Flying,* and *The Road to Wigan Pier* by George Orwell are reprinted by permission of Harcourt Brace Jovanovich, Inc.

Excerpts from *Homage to Catalonia* by George Orwell, copyright 1952, 1980 by Sonia Brownell Orwell. Reprinted by permission of Harcourt Brace Jovanovich, Inc.

Excerpts from *Nineteen Eighty-Four* by George Orwell, copyright 1949 by Harcourt Brace Jovanovich, Inc.; renewed 1977 by Sonia Brownell Orwell. Reprinted by permission of the publisher.

Excerpts from *The Collected Essays, Journalism and Letters of George Orwell,* copyright © 1968 by Sonia Brownell Orwell. Reprinted by permission of Harcourt Brace Jovanovich, Inc.

George Orwell in Wallington Churchyard, Hertfordshire, England, 1939 (photo courtesy of Denis Collings, George Orwell Archive, London).

CHRONOLOGY: GEORGE ORWELL'S LIFE AND WORKS

1903   25 June, Eric Arthur Blair (later George Orwell) born at Motihari, Bengal, India. Only son of Ida Mabel Limouzin and Richard Walmesley Blair, subdeputy agent in the Opium Department of the Indian Civil Service.

1904   Ida Blair returns to England with Eric and his older sister, Marjorie.

1911   Enters St. Cyprian's preparatory school.

1914   Patriotic poem in *Henley and South Thames Oxfordshire Standard*.

1916   Completes studies at St. Cyprian's.

1917   Enters Eton as a member of the King's Scholars, an intellectually elite group. Contributes short stories and satirical verse to the *Election Times* and *College Days*.

1921   Leaves Eton; low academic rank makes a scholarship to Oxford virtually impossible.

1922   Passes examination for Imperial Indian Police; sent to police training school in Rangoon, Burma, as assistant superintendent of police.

1927   Resigns from Imperial Service while on leave in England.

1928   In spring travels to Paris to become writer while living in a working-class district. Enters a Paris hospital because of pneumonia.

1929   Returns to England.

1930   Begins contributing book reviews to *New Adelphi* (later *Adelphi*) while spending time among tramps, picking hops in Kent, and tutoring.

1932   Teaches in small private school from April 1932 until December 1933.

1933   *Down and Out in Paris and London.* Enters Uxbridge hospital in November with pneumonia.

1934   Moves to London; becomes part-time assistant at Booklovers' Corner, a Hampstead bookshop, in October; *Burmese Days* published in the United States.

1935   *A Clergyman's Daughter* and *Burmese Days* published in England; begins submitting articles and reviews to *New English Weekly.*

1936   *Keep the Aspidistra Flying.* Moves to the Stores, Wallington, Hertfordshire. Marries Eileen O'Shaughnessy in June. Travels to Barcelona, Spain.

1937   Participates in Spanish Civil War. *The Road to Wigan Pier* published in March. Wounded in the throat by enemy sniper in May. Leaves Spain in July for Wallington.

1938   Suffers a tubercular lesion in one lung in March and is confined to a sanatarium in Kent until September. Travels with Eileen to Morocco. *Homage to Catalonia* published in April. Joins Independent Labor party in June.

1939   Returns to England in March. *Coming Up for Air* published in June. Fails in attempt to join army.

1940   Returns to London in May; joins Home Guard batallion in June. *Inside the Whale* published in March.

1941   First of his "London Letters" articles published in *Partisan Review. The Lion and the Unicorn.* Joins Indian section of the BBC Far Eastern Service. Two essays appear as chapters in *The Betrayal of the Left.*

1943   Mother dies in March. Leaves Home Guard in November for reasons of health; resigns from BBC and later becomes literary editor of the *Tribune.* Begins reviewing books for the *Manchester Evening News.*

1944   *Animal Farm* submitted to and rejected by Gollancz, Jonathan Cape, Faber & Faber, and a number of American publishers before it is accepted by Secker & Warburg. The Blairs adopt infant boy in June.

1945   Eileen dies during surgery. *Animal Farm* published in August.

1946   *Critical Essays* (in America *Dickens, Dali and Others*) published in February.

1947   Falls ill in April; enters Hairmyres Hospital near Glasgow in December.

Chronology

1948	First volume of Secker & Warburg uniform edition of writings appears in May. Returns from hospital to Barnhill. Completes *Nineteen Eighty-Four* in early December.
1949	Enters Cotswold (Gloucestershire) Sanatarium in January. *Nineteen Eighty-Four* published in June. Moves to University College Hospital in London in September. Marries Sonia Brownell in October.
1950	Dies 21 January, buried in Berkshire at Sutton Courtenay churchyard.

1

HISTORICAL CONTEXT

The England that George Orwell returned to in December 1929 after having spent most of the previous eight years abroad, mainly in the East, was a complex society holding on to traditional ways of thought and behavior even while undergoing unprecedented changes, a society of material luxury for some but poverty for many. Legislation in the areas of education, health, housing, and insurance was to some extent diminishing the prewar gap between the living conditions of the upper classes and those of the lower classes—the notorious two nations of Victorian social thought. In the South and the Midlands new industries geared for the mass production of goods—luxury items as well as necessities—were becoming as economically important to the British economy as were the older industries of the North. In 1929 the Liberal party—successor to the Whigs, the party of Gladstone and Lloyd George—lost the General Election to the Labor party and thereby its role as a major force in British politics—its place as the main opposition to the Conservatives being taken by Labor. And since the mid-1920s, Britain's rate of economic growth had passed that of the years before the recent war.

In some ways, however, England maintained its traditions. The leadership of the nation—its politicians and civil servants, its businessmen and professionals—was still being drawn mainly from the middle and upper middle classes. Despite educational reforms, most young people did not continue their education full-time after elementary school, and higher education was still mainly for children of the upper classes. And even though some of the more visible class differences were being planed away, there was still a great disparity between the income levels of the upper and lower classes. Despite economic growth, unemployment remained high, especially in the North.

In Europe economic turmoil was having ominous political consequences. In October 1922, the same month that Orwell set sail for India, Italian Blackshirts, fascist followers of Benito Mussolini, staged their "March on Rome," which resulted in the fall of the liberal-democratic government and Mussolini's accession to power. In 1927, the year of Orwell's return from the East, Adolph Hitler's *Mein Kampf* was published, and the Communist party Congress of the Soviet Union, supporting Stalin's emphasis on socialism at home, overwhelmingly rejected the call of his rival, Leon Trotsky, for world revolution and later expelled him from the Soviet Union. Nineteen thirty-three, the year that Orwell completed his first published novel, was also the first year of Hitler's chancellorship. In 1935, when Orwell started on *Keep the Aspidistra Flying*, the protagonist of which spends most of his time avoiding gainful employment, a Soviet miner named Stakhanov so markedly increased his daily production of coal that he and later Stakhanovites became official Soviet heroes.

For more than a decade and a half the English people, as well as many of their leaders, paid more attention to domestic or colonial affairs than to developments in Europe. However, the events of 1936 drew England's attention across the channel and set Orwell on his future course as a writer. In March Hitler moved German troops into the Rhineland, an act in contravention of the 1919 treaty ending World War I, and in July General Francisco Franco led a military rebellion against the recently elected Popular Front Spanish government—a civil war that eventually pitted antifascist volunteers from Europe, England, and the Americas against well-equipped units from fascist Italy and Nazi Germany. From the mid-thirties on, the authoritarian governments acted quickly: Italy and Germany became allies in 1936, later including Japan, which, then controlled by right-wing military elements, attacked China in 1937, the same year that Germany violated another provision of the peace treaty by taking control of the free city of Danzig. In 1938 Germany annexed Austria; in 1939, after having occupied the predominantly German-speaking Sudentenland, Hitler's armies invaded non-German Czechoslovakia, and Italy invaded Albania. To the anger and disillusionment of many people sympathetic to communism, Stalin signed a nonaggression pact with Germany in August 1939—a move that was supposed to enable Hitler to concentrate his forces in the West. World War II began on 1 September 1939 when Germany invaded Poland, thereby forcing France and England, bound by treaty to defend Poland, to declare war—referred to as a "phoney war" until Hitler attacked in Western Europe the following April.

Despite significant theoretical differences not only between communism and the two right-wing ideologies of fascism and Nazism but also between the latter two, these systems do share traits important to an understanding of the mood of the thirties, the period of Orwell's political education.

As organized revolutionary movements, all three were dramatic responses to massive economic turmoil and human suffering more or less directly connected with World War I and its aftermath. In place of ministerial caution and parliamentary debate, the new parties offered quick, forceful action—action often not hampered by constitutional or legal niceties—to restore order. Mass movements whose leaders intended to establish a strong central government exercising an iron control over just about every aspect of social and certainly political life, these new systems of rule were avowed enemies of liberalism, with its advocacy of limited government, freedom for the individual, and other values associated with the historical development of bourgeois civilization. The creation of the total state involved a more or less extensive period of social conflict and divisiveness, including violence, as Aryan eliminated or subjugated non-Aryan and the proletariat eradicated all traces of capitalism and capitalists. From the standpoint of European parliamentary democracy, these were extremist movements—revolutionary rather than reformist, rigidly doctrinaire, anti-pluralist, and hostile to compromise. Hostile, too, to Christianity, they came to be regarded as secular religions offering their followers a discipline, a philosophy, and a cause for which to live and die.

Even though these foreign ideologies—foreign, too, in the sense of being incompatible with the hard-earned English respect for moderation and compromise—never gained much ground in Britain, traditional liberalism continued to suffer a loss of prestige as the capitalist economic system with which it was associated seemed to be entering the final stage of its decline. Increasingly important were various noncommunist forms of socialism, and one in particular—Fabian socialism—exercised a marked influence on the policies and programs of the British Labor party. Founded in 1884, the Fabian Society, although never a large group, included such popular and articulate figures as George Bernard Shaw and H. G. Wells. The society's proposals for gradual and limited reforms were based on detailed, empirical research—as set forth in public lectures, publications, and summer schools—rather than on dogmatic assertions.

Largely because of their sociological interests, Wells and, to some extent, Shaw drifted to the edge of the literary mainstream in the twenties—the decade of the modernists (James Joyce, Virginia Woolf, D. H. Lawrence, T. S. Eliot) whose field of imaginative activity was primarily the inner self. To the modernist, the proper aim of the serious artist should be the convincing presentation of mental experience, including the workings of the unconscious mind, and external reality—the world of material objects, physical action, public events—was considered artistically valuable insofar as it could be translated into the symbolically evocative language of intuition, reverie, and dream.

The overall impression given by the modernist movement was of an artistic community unresponsive to the social crises of the age.

In the nineteen-thirties appeared a generation of writers who, as England's economic situation visibly worsened and darkening masses of political thunderheads moved westward across Europe, began to emphasize the social and political responsibility of art. Although mainly from liberal, middle-class, and professional backgrounds and educated in the better schools, most of the writers and intellectuals who turned their talents toward public issues did so as leftist progressives inscribing the epitaph of a moribund bourgeois civilization. Poets figured prominently in the early stages of this trend, the leader and widely imitated model being the Oxford-educated physician's son W. H. Auden. While using modernist techniques to explore into the collective psyche of capitalist society, Auden and others developed an early postmodernist rhetoric comprised of extraliterary concepts (such as Marxism), cinematic techniques, and popular subliterary forms— including ballad, nursery rime, doggerel verse, and music hall song. Later in the thirties, when fiction writers were exploiting the narrative potential of the poets' England as symbolic landscape, the popular adventure thriller was used for serious purposes. Two motifs, one conceptual and the other structural, became important—neurosis, that of a whole society, and the journey-quest. From the former was developed the metaphor of Europe as an insane asylum with the most dangerous inmates in control; from the latter, the metaphor of the frontier, the borderland between a known and charted past and a future of massive change. The literature of the thirties, like the age itself, tended toward extremes—either the extreme of nonrealistic art (allegory, beast fable, satiric fantasy) or the opposite extreme of the documentary.

With its late Victorian, naturalistic realism and atmosphere of individual isolation and futility, Orwell's early published fiction bears little similarity to the literary experimentation of his leftist contemporaries. The obsessed and self-tormenting protagonists of his first three novels owe more to Dickens and Dostoyevski than to Marx.

However, Orwell's association with the leftist magazine *Adelphi* and later with the even more left-wing publishing house of Victor Gollancz increased his social awareness. After Orwell's return from Spain, the need vividly to convey the political enormities of the age led him to engage in literary experimentation—such as the use of the satiric allegorical beast fable in *Animal Farm* and the combination Gothic melodrama and dystopian novel in *Nineteen Eighty-Four*.

2
THE IMPORTANCE OF
THE WORK

Since its initial publication in England by Secker & Warburg and in the United States by Harcourt, Brace, *Animal Farm* has been read by millions throughout the world. Later editions have been issued by such prestigious publishing houses as Heinemann and Longman's, Green. Samuel French Publications issued a two-act dramatic version of *Animal Farm*, and in 1984 a stage musical adaptation (published by Methuen) opened at the National Theatre, London, and later played in Finland, Spain, Austria, Switzerland, Canada, and the United States. The performance this writer attended at the Olivier auditorium of the National Theatre in January 1987 drew a large audience, despite the fact that it was on an evening during a spell of cold weather reported to have been the harshest since the early 1940s. Moreover, editions of the book have appeared in the following foreign languages: Afrikaans, Danish, Dutch, Finnish, French, German, Greek, Icelandic, Indonesian, Italian, Maltese, Norwegian, Polish, Portuguese, Serbo-Croatian, Sinhalese, Czech, Slovene, Spanish, Swahili, Swedish, Ukrainian, and Vietnamese. Banned in the Soviet Union and Eastern European countries except Yugoslavia, *Animal Farm* has circulated in prohibited areas in the form of illegal *samizdat* editions.

The popularity of a work of art is one sign of its importance, and one reason for the mass appeal of *Animal Farm* is the classic simplicity of its language and style—an English as understandable to the adolescent as to the adult. With the exception of a few unusual terms—the colloquial "knackers" and the technical "coccidiosis"—the vocabulary is ordinary and commonplace without being so basic and limited as to be interesting only to children. Similarly, Orwell's sentences follow a structural middle course. Although there are a few simple, single-clause sentences and some that are compound-complex (having at least two main clauses and at least one subordinate clause), most are simply compound sentences, composed of two, sometimes more, main clauses. In its general effect, Orwell's style of writing in *Animal Farm* is nonhierarchical and egalitarian. And despite its simplicity, the language is flexible enough to convey a range of conditions and attitudes—from the unadorned descriptions of Clover's solicitude to the intellectual abstractness of Snowball's Latinate vocabulary, from the pathetic earnestness of Boxer's uplift slogans to Squealer's molasses-smooth sophistries.

Another important quality of *Animal Farm,* a trait connected with its disarming simplicity, is its imaginative power. One line of action dominates—the course of the animals' experiment in self-rule from the initial rebellion against their negligent owner, Farmer Jones, to their struggles to establish a stable and independent society and finally to the sobering estrangement of the porcine leaders from the humbler beasts. But here and there along this parabola are brief, often unexpected scenes that grip and hold our attention for an instant before we are drawn back into the forward momentum of the narrative—now a charming tableau of animal gentleness, now a nightmarish spectacle of hysteria and rage. Although lacking the wealth of physical detail to be found in Jonathan Swift's *Gulliver's Travels*, to which Orwell's work has been compared, and the imagistic density of Orwell's earlier fiction, *Animal Farm* uses its sparser imagery to good effect in terms of compactness and unity. Windows bracket the story of the revolution—the window from which an angry Farmer Jones fires his gun while the animals experience their first moment of political excitement, and at the end the window through which the humbler beasts that have survived the years of austerity, drudgery, and oppressive rule witness the disfiguring rancor of the leader from whose values and behavior they are estranged. This and other motifs—repeated references to alcohol, the windmill, Boxer's optimistic slogans, to name a few more—resonate throughout the narrative, sometimes producing ironic dissonance, sometimes sounding deep chords of primal emotions and archetypal aspirations.

It is interesting to note that the most memorable feature of the book—the final revision of the animals' revolutionary commandments: "ALL ANIMALS ARE EQUAL BUT SOME ANIMALS ARE MORE EQUAL THAN OTHERS"—is not entirely original with Orwell, for an earlier statement of this idea, with markedly similar wording, appeared in "A Russian Fairy Tale," a short anti-Soviet fable by the British writer Philip Guedalla published in 1930 in *The Missing Muse*.[1] However, whether Orwell's sentence is a borrowing or a coincidental restatement, the point is that it is Orwell's phrasing—phrasing made more poignant by the peculiarly Orwellian context of narrative events and feelings—that survives. In fact, around this statement as around the book has crystallized a complex of attitudes and judgments about twentieth-century political activism. For good or ill, there must be many thousands of individuals throughout the noncommunist world whose conception of the Russian Revolution and the Stalin era bears the stamp of Orwell's fable.

The ability of *Animal Farm* to survive as a piece of literature, to engage the imagination and emotions of future readers, may well depend on an expanded awareness of the work as an integral part of a much larger cultural fabric, its interwoven strands extending from the ancient past. The multihued threads of *Animal Farm*—satire, various allegorical forms, myth, animal story, fairy tale, morality, ballad, lamentation, and others—are traceable through the English-language classics of Dickens, Poe, Swift, Gay, Dryden, Bunyan, Shakespeare, Spenser, and Chaucer, and across the channel to the Brothers Grimm and La Fontaine, and further back to Ovid, Aesop, Aristophanes, Homer, the Gospel of Matthew, the Book of Isaiah, and farther east to the Sanskrit *Panchatantra* and the Buddhist *jatakas*. Any broadening of a reader's perspective helps to reveal *Animal Farm* as not simply an isolated literary phenomenon relevant only to a particular moment in history but also a cell contributing to the ongoing life of a civilizing literary tradition.

3

CRITICAL RECEPTION

Before examining the critical response to *Animal Farm* from the mid-1940s to the present, it will be helpful to note Orwell's explanation of his intentions in writing the book. To the extent that political factors contributed to his decision to write this particular book at a certain time, the most detailed explanatory statement is contained in a translation back into English of Orwell's preface to the émigré Ukrainian edition of *Animal Farm* (1947)—this preface having been written in March 1947, three years after the completion of the original work. The preface reveals two guiding impulses behind the fable. The more fully stated motive is active and aggressive—to destroy Westerners' illusions about the Soviet Union (in the 1940s under the control of Joseph Stalin in his dual capacity as premier and general secretary of the Communist party) by exposing the falsity of claims that the Soviet Union was a socialist and therefore progressive society. Here it should be pointed out that in the Marxist-Leninist view of contemporary revolutionary history, the term socialism refers to the penultimate stage of human progress, a period of sociopolitical reorganization and reeducation following the collapse of capitalism and bourgeois democracy and preceding the establishment of a full-fledged and permanent communist society. The type of rule during the socialist phase was to be a dictatorship of the proletariat, the industrial working class. For Orwell and other socialists unsympathetic to this formulation, socialism was to be neither dictatorial nor temporary, but rather democratic and permanent.

If the wording of the retranslated preface accurately reflects the original, Orwell's other impulse appears to have been simultaneously prophylactic and restorative—to prevent democratic socialists from being taken in by the Marxist-Leninist definition of socialism and thereby to assist in the recuperation of an ailing Western European socialist movement.[2] A fuller statement regarding the latter aim—Orwell's intention to aid authentic socialism—appears in an article published while he was in the middle of writing *Animal Farm*. Here his aim is to establish the defensible perimeter of a viable socialism by ceding the indefensible never-never land of utopianist aspiration to another threatening force—ideologically reactionary "neo-pessimists" eager to use any shortcoming in the actual practice of socialism to debunk the whole movement. The claim that a perfect society is inevitable under socialism is, Orwell asserts, a straw man set up to be knocked down by socialism's enemies on the right. To counter the do-nothing attitude produced by such pessimism, it is important to emphasize that a socialist society would certainly not be perfect, nor would it offer much to satisfy the needs of a hedonist. The only promise that true socialism is permitted to make is to improve society by righting "economic injustice."[3]

An important aspect of the early reviews is their stated or implied presupposition about the approaches to *Animal Farm*. Descriptions and assessments are based on the assumption that Orwell's allegorical fable is—or is meant to be—historically referential, that it is a more or less direct reflection of significant political events, situations, and even specific figures associated with the history of the Soviet Union from the two 1917 revolutions to the 1940s, with the German invasion of Russian and Stalin's meeting with the Allied leaders at Teheran. Another assumption is that *Animal Farm* is to be taken seriously as philosophically or attitudinally expressive, that it reflects Orwell's considered judgment on either revolutionary activism in general or utopian planning. Assessments resting on the first assumption, the referential nature of the work, tend to emphasize its identity as an allegorical fable, although in many cases the evaluations of its success or failure appear to have been based less on formal literary factors than on the point-for-point accuracy or inaccuracy of its thinly veiled portrayal of Eastern European social and diplomatic history. Apart from an occasional quibble regarding the work's referential precision—one reviewer wondered what group in the Soviet Union the ill-starred Boxer represented,[4] and another critic noted the absence of a Lenin figure[5]—most reviewers and critics have accepted the parallelism of fiction and referent. Nearly everyone who has written on *Animal Farm* has mentioned the historical parallels, but Jeffrey Meyers, J. R. Hammond, and Lutz Buethe have supplied the most comprehensive lists of referents, a conflation of which follows.

Farmer Jones is Czar Nicholas II, overthrown by the revolution and later executed by the Bolsheviks; Old Major is Marx and perhaps Marxist-Leninism; Boxer and Clover represent the proletariat (the urban industrial worker)—and more remotely the Chinese revolutionaries of the 1900 Boxer Rebellion; Napoleon stands for Joseph Stalin; Snowball is Leon Trotsky; Mollie is at heart a White Russian with little sympathy for Bolshevik aims; the raven Moses stands for the Russian Orthodox church and to a lesser extent the Roman Catholic church, with which at one time Stalin imagined he could reach an accord; Squealer is *Pravda,* official organ of the Communist party in the Soviet Union, and the pigs in general represent the party; Farmer Pilkington stands for Churchillian England, while Farmer Frederick is Hitler Germany; the animal uprising is the 1917 Revolution (actually two revolutions); the so-called battles of the Cowshed and the Windmill are, respectively, the early Western military intervention in support of White Russian resistance to the Bolsheviks and the 1941 invasion of the Soviet Union by German forces; the building of the windmill corresponds to Stalin's various five-year plans for rapid industrialization (although similar plans were instituted also in Hitler Germany); Jones's farmhouse becomes the Kremlin, seat of the Soviet government; the slaughter by Napoleon's dogs of fellow animals supposedly working for Snowball-Trotsky are the bloody Moscow purge trials, mainly of the 1930s; Stalin's dealings with the treacherous Frederick recalls the nonaggression pact between Hitler Germany and the Soviet Union; and the continued drudgery imposed on the worker animals is likened to Stalin's policy of forced collectivization.[6]

Over the years it has become commonplace for interpreters of Orwell to emphasize the anti-Soviet bias of *Animal Farm*, seeing the primary aim and effect of the work as a satiric exposure of the failings and horrors of the Soviet system and a blackening of the favorable image of Stalinist Russia current in some Western circles.[7] However, from the start *Animal Farm*—and the authorial outlook and attitude inferred from it—has generated the strongest reactions, negative as well as positive, from readers. The Orwell who, as indicated above, claimed while the book was in progress that he wanted to protect socialism from right-wing nay-sayers later became the biter bit, for since then a number of reviewers and critics have called attention to the work's pessimistic vision of politics and life. And arising out of the view of Orwell—the Orwellian Orwell emergent in the 1940s—as satirist of leftist revolutionary activism was the question of Orwell's real attitude toward socialism (a matter of greater moment to the British than to Americans). This issue was raised by an early reviewer who saw in the narrative's treatment of Snowball—a Trotsky rendered politically impotent in the fable—as Orwell's implicit rejection of socialism itself.[8] However, in one of the first extensive treatments of Orwell's oeuvre, John Atkins maintains that although *Animal Farm* is primarily an "attack on Stalinism . . . it is an attack from the Left"—a "Socialist's mockery" of a nonsocialist Soviet Union.[9] But just as emphatic in its interpretation of the book's antisocialist picture of the common people's incapacity for self-rule is a later critique.[10] And the

Critical Reception

Animal Farm discussed in Alex Zwerdling's book-length study of Orwell's relationship to British left-wing thought is ambiguous in its attitude toward socialism.[11]

At this point it will be useful to step back from the specifics of early Orwell criticism to note a peculiar development related to Orwell's reputation—a reputation based as much upon his image as a social and political commentator as on his qualities as literary artist. Orwell's opening sentence in the 1940 essay "Charles Dickens"—that "Dickens is one of those writers who are well worth stealing"—portended Orwell's fate after the publication of *Nineteen Eighty-Four* and his death.[12] As the writer of a *Time* magazine cover story on Orwell put it: "The impulse to hold Orwell's coat while sending his ghost out to battle now [in 1983] seems pandemic."[13] Probably no Western novelist since Dickens has aroused so strong a competition among representatives of various sociopolitical ideologies and tendencies to claim the man as an adherent. By much the same token, toward few modern writers has there been such negative criticism—some extreme, some valid—from individuals and groups made bitter by his exasperating habit of stepping out of ranks in which he had lined up at one time or another. From one perspective, *Animal Farm* has been viewed as marking Orwell's abandonment of progressive principles developed during the thirties when the enemy was Nazism and fascism. From another perspective, *Animal Farm* (and later *Nineteen Eighty-Four*) betokens its author's refusal to permit an autonomous man's inconsistencies and ambiguities to be regimented into a fixed and unwavering vision of reality. In recent years so-called neoconservatives have most forcefully argued for Orwell as a rock-hard antileftist, his stony gaze bifocally fixed on Eastern European commissar and Western fellow traveler.[14] So established has this partisan image of Orwell become that during the *annus Orwelliensis*, 1984, appeared a collection of essays with a leftist point of view and concerned mainly with questioning the "*Myth*" (the key word of the book's title) of a socialist Orwell.[15]

Some early reviewers judged the work's indirect depiction of revolutionary Russia to be unfairly harsh, one writer complaining that it was "calculated . . . to fill the hearts of . . . sincere and realistic idealists everywhere with the blackest despair."[16] Orwell's satire came to be perceived as a Cassandra cry for any revolutionary activism. Although some writers have seen Orwell's satire as restricted to the Russian revolution, not infrequently the book has been regarded as being radically antirevolutionary—its message being that the "ideals of justice, equality, and fraternity always shatter" in a revolutionary situation,[17] that disaster must result from "political action of any kind and in pursuit of any ostensible aim."[18]

Although *Nineteen Eighty-Four* is commonly regarded as Orwell's most detailed examination and most vivid dramatization of power hunger as a key factor in the emergence of totalitarianism, critics have noted the presence of power hunger as a theme and object of satire in *Animal Farm*. Somewhat less controversial an issue than Orwell's socialism, the depiction of the quest for political power and the consequences of that craving have been accorded the magisterial sweep of Lord Acton's generalization about the universally corrupting effect of power. In the mid-fifties Christopher Hollis described the range of Orwell's satire as broad enough to include conservative greed along with communist tyranny,[19] and a later critic insisted on the relevance of the fable's message to the British Tory readiness to make self-serving accommodations with leftist dictatorships.[20] Not the total control aimed at by the Soviet system alone but totalitarianism of any stripe is corrupting.[21]

Given the 1930s' legacy of political excitement that carried over to Orwell's work in the forties, the emphasis by reviewers and critics on the political intentionality of *Animal Farm* was to be expected, and, as Orwell could have predicted, particular interpretations of his writings, especially of *Animal Farm* and *Nineteen Eighty-Four*, have been tied to stated or implied judgments not infrequently reflecting the political inclination of the interpreter. A notable example of this is the attack on *Animal Farm* by the Irish playwright Sean O'Casey, nationalistic and semicommunistic celebrant of the common folk, generated by anger at what he regarded as the depiction of the worker-animals as collectively helpless.[22]

Emphasizing a paraphrasable meaning or supposed authorial attitude that is first abstracted from the narrative and then judged in terms of *this* social philosophy or *that* political leaning might obscure the artistic presence of the work, its existence as an imaginative construct. Although Orwell was either recognizing an inescapable general truth of the age or simply setting himself up as a target in claiming during the 1940s that all art is propagandistic,[23] in an essay published in the summer of 1946, "Why I Write," he claimed to have been motivated over the preceding ten years by a desire to "make political writing into an art" and stated that in *Animal Farm* he had for the first time in his writing career consciously tried to achieve this goal— to harmonize political concerns with artistry.[24] From the recognition of the work's aesthetic dimension, its identity as a literary artifact, have developed several important critical practices and approaches. The most general of these involves the recognition that *Animal Farm* is made up of a number of literary genres (a term more or less synonymous with type, form, and mode), such as satire and fairy tale, and such subtypes as the allegorical fable and parable. The number of authoritative works on literary types and modes that refer to *Animal Farm* suggests the importance it has achieved in terms of various literary traditions.[25]

A clearer idea of the literary classifications applicable to *Animal Farm* has made possible a genre criticism of the work, with associated literary concepts the matrices of interpretation and evaluations. In an early review of *Animal Farm*, Northrop Frye, who was later to write one of the most influential books on literary classification (*Anatomy of Criticism*, 1957), based his criticism on genre. Frye argued that because the work relies on one of the "classical formulas of satire," the "corruption of principle by expediency," *Animal Farm* misses its mark, since the degeneration of the Russian Revolution resulted from the opposite process—expediency, in the sense of an empirical approach to reality, having been transformed into principle, an abstract metaphysics.[26] The importance of a genre approach is underscored by its use in relation to one of the most controversial issues in Orwell criticism—the nature, extent, and implications of pessimism as a tonal element in *Animal Farm*.

Although Frye criticized Orwell for allowing a standard satiric motif to control the thematic content of *Animal Farm*, other critics—mainly those dissatisfied with the work's supposed antiprogressive bias, with what has been regarded as an atmosphere of inevitable defeat hanging over the animals' idealistic endeavors—have focused on the work as a beast fable. Early in the 1950s an influential critic complained that in using animals to represent the working class, Orwell was implying the political ineffectiveness of all workers;[27] a longtime friend of Orwell was distressed by an animal-worker equation that placed the latter at an "irremediable disadvantage in the class struggle";[28] and given the limited mental capacity of the bulk of the farm animals in the fable, it has been regarded as inevitable that they should be easy marks for the more intelligent pigs.[29] A related criticism appearing from the forties to the eighties is that the fable form simplifies a complex historical situation and thus precludes an insightful, politically sophisticated examination of its subject matter.[30]

Some critics of Orwell have examined the form and structure of *Animal Farm* while muting or suspending judgments on the political and ideological implications of its literary devices. Worth noting in this respect is the suggestion in a 1960 edition of the novel made by Laurence Brander, author of one of the earliest books on Orwell. Perhaps reacting to the atmosphere of cold war partisanship hardening around Orwell criticism in the 1950s, Brander proposed that the work be appreciated for its literary narrative qualities—appreciated not because of its political message but because of its entertaining story based on the animals' interactions.[31]

Even if later criticism insisted on dealing with the political intentions of *Animal Farm*, an increasing number of critics has accepted the political content as a given in order to assess more fully the literary and rhetorical effectiveness of the work's techniques. Later in the sixties attention was paid to the beast fable as a means of controlling the direction of the satire or of intensifying the reader's emotional reaction to the objects of satire,[32] and more recently the fable form has been credited with giving the narrative a timelessness and universality.[33] A few critics have dealt with *Animal Farm* as a fairy tale, in keeping with its Secker & Warburg subtitle, and several have related that form to a bipolarizing separation of the pigs, trapped in an evil world of frightening metamorphoses, from the humbler animals, whose collective goodness endures.[34] Another critic has interpreted the fairy-tale elements as a warning to the reader not to accept magical explanations for political events.[35] An approach based on the literary type known as pastoral, often celebrating man's closeness to nature but in *Animal Farm* shown as being disrupted by the intrusion of power politics, is employed by yet another critic.[36]

One of the more firmly rooted assessments of Orwell, literary as well as biographical, common amongst critics is that of the author as a singular, solitary figure, a literary loner, with a maverick vision of contemporary reality. This view has been balanced, however, by two related trends in Orwell criticism: the comparison of Orwell as political thinker and writer to such important contemporaries as Ignazio Silone and Arthur Koestler,[37] and the placement of Orwell within literary traditions based upon the work of earlier writers. The second trend has been more closely associated with *Animal Farm* than has the first; both the specific devices in the novel and its general spirit can be traced back to Edwardian, Victorian, and earlier writers especially favored by Orwell. Orwell's own reviews and essays clearly reveal his enduring interest in the fiction of H. G. Wells, Rudyard Kipling, Charles Dickens, and Jonathan Swift. Several works of criticism examine in detail the literary relationship between *Animal Farm* and other writers.[38] Although *Animal Farm* is sometimes regarded as tonally consistent with the social or political pessimism attributed to Orwell's other works, technical discussions of it tend not to connect it with Orwell's earlier narratives. Whether praised for its artistry or faulted for superficiality, *Animal Farm* has been regarded as somewhat marginal to Orwell's general development as a writer.[39]

Mention should be made of critical developments of the late seventies and eighties. The absurdist function of the satiric technique of *Animal Farm* is the subject of a German critic's article,[40] and the functional relationship between the use of particular verbal formulas and the thematic content of *Animal Farm* is part of another German scholar's book-length study of Orwell's linguistic habits.[41] Emphasis is placed on the purposeful fictionality of *Animal Farm*, the intentional disparity between animal narrative and historical reality, as an example of Orwell's effort throughout his writing career to establish a rhetorical "stance" permitting an effective author-work-reader interaction.[42] A feminist critic recently interpreted *Animal Farm* as Orwell's questioning of his own patriarchal attitudes.[43]

Detailed background information on the writing of *Animal Farm* and Orwell's attempts to find a publisher for it are contained in Bernard Crick's biography.[44] To some extent supplementing the relevant correspondence in volume 4 of the *Collected Essays* is a recent collection of ten letters sent by Orwell to his literary agent in regard to *Animal Farm*.[45] The most recent contributions to the background of *Animal Farm* and influences on Orwell's thinking in the early forties are the companion volumes of his wartime BBC broadcasts and commentaries.[46]

A READING

4

—— INTRODUCTION

In stating in "Why I Write" that since around the mid-1930s he had
been attempting to convey political themes in an artistically satisfying
manner, Orwell reveals himself to have been a writer very much of the
age. Given the fact that during this period not only was literature
being politicized but also writers, intellectuals, and politicians were
being identified and evaluated in terms of their ideological positions,
there is at least a touch of the allegorically symbolic in the rough reception awaiting the manuscript of *Animal Farm* in 1944—from the
slings of the intellectual left (its terse rejection by the leftist publisher
Victor Gollancz) to the arrows of the militaristic right (a German
bomb that "blitzed" Orwell's apartment and buried the manuscript
under a pile of rubble).[47] *Animal Farm* is, in other words, the age writ
small. Woven into the fabric of this apparently simple narrative are
not only thoughts and feelings about the sociopolitical tensions of the
last few years but, more broadly, complex attitudes and ideas concern-
ing England's historical development from its Victorian and agricultural past into an age of mechanization and mass ideologies. Another

way to conceive of the novel's hidden complexity is to view it three-dimensionally: in the foreground is the immediate object of satire, the totalitarian features of Soviet society under Stalin; in the middle distance is Orwell's uneasiness about the future of socialism; and the larger background is an abiding concern—by the 1940s almost an obsession—with the condition of England past, present, and future.

An assumption basic to the present study is that a reader's appreciation of the thematic richness and tonal depth of *Animal Farm* can be enhanced by viewing the novel within the context of Orwell's development as writer and thinker—a development linked to his perception of events and conditions inside England and beyond its shores that were widening the gap between past and present. The tracing of lines connecting *Animal Farm* with the Orwellian literary personality of the 1940s, itself an outgrowth of and reaction to the Orwell of the 1930s, involves an examination of several different groups of writings: first, both Orwell's fiction and nonfiction, with emphasis on writings that appeared at around the same time that he was working on *Animal Farm*; second, those writings and writers with which and whom Orwell was certainly familiar, as indicated by his own references to them; and also works that probably influenced his thought and imagination, directly or subtly—works (or types of writings) perhaps known to Orwell because of his lifelong interest in imaginative literature or adult interest in contemporary events, or simply because they were in his personal library.

Although Orwell's reading was too varied to allow for absolute generalizations about the literary factors shaping his mind and imagination—his tastes ran from James Joyce and Shakespeare to Fabian pamphlets and obscure seventeenth-century tracts—some writers and writings left a clear imprint on his thinking. Repeatedly Orwell called attention to his fascination with *Gulliver's Travels*: whatever may have been the appeal of Swift's puritanism and antihedonism, certainly Orwell was touched by the Irishman's sensitivity to dishonesty and injustice. Equally inspiring was Charles Dickens's ability to transform imaginatively personal outrage at social injustice into powerful literary images.

Introduction

The specific aim of this study is to examine the dual nature of *Animal Farm*, its bipolar orientation. On the one hand, the work calls to the attention of the contemporary reader some of the most alarming realities of a politically violent century; on the other, it offers readers an opportunity to become more emotionally and imaginatively receptive to valuable apolitical modes of experience—experience intimately connected with the reader's personal and social past. The historical past to which *Animal Farm* is designed to sensitize its readers is what Orwell considered to be on the whole the more vital, emotionally healthy, and socially cohesive and trusting world of premodern, preindustrial England—an agricultural society whose members lived in closer harmony with organic reality and natural rhythms. *Animal Farm* is doing—or attempting to do, more or less successfully—two things: at the same time that the narrative is drawing the reader into the politically satirical allegory, conjuring up scenes that hold the reader in thrall to the fable's indirect presentation of disturbing public realities, the story is also evoking in the reader's mind a sense of a prepolitical self—intimations of a pastoral identity somewhere deep within the modern psyche.

The political theme of *Animal Farm* is closely associated with its satiric tone and its form as allegorical fable; the pastoral spirit of the work—its fleeting glimpses of a bucolic, somewhat idealized but not necessarily utopian rural existence—bears some kinship to the nonpoliticized animal story of the adult reader's childhood, if not his actual past. Although the English social novel has a long history, the political novel is a relatively recent phenomenon in Britain, and the tension between political message and pastoral sensibility in *Animal Farm* certainly reflects Orwell's uneasiness with the demands made by contemporary public crises on the private imagination and probably reflects the ambivalence of other British writers. Several years after writing *Animal Farm,* Orwell claimed that money used to buy rose bushes for planting was "better spent" than money for even an "excellent" Fabian research pamphlet.[48] Of the four motives for his own writing listed in "Why I Write"—personal expression, aesthetic pleasure, the accurate description of external reality, and political persuasion—the first two are clearly nonpolitical, the third—termed a "historical impulse"—could easily relate to public matters, and the last, the wish to exert some influence on world developments, is clearly political in intention and, it is suggested, widespread in literature. And the point stressed here is that these motives "must war against one another." The fact that in describing his work in *Animal Farm* Orwell claims only that this was the first time he had ever consciously "attempted" to unify some of these warring impulses[49] raises the interesting possibility that this novel—rather than being a nearly finished, classically marmoreal piece of sterile perfection—is a living work still warm from its own inner conflicts and those of the age from which it was generated.

Since the examination of the relationship of *Animal Farm* to its sociopolitical and cultural context will involve an identification not simply of ideas but also images and motifs contributing to the development of Orwell's imaginative and intellectual vision of reality at mid-century, a brief survey of the literary influences emphasized in this study, including Orwell's own writings, is in order. Among the important political writers with whose works Orwell gained some degree of familiarity as a reviewer (and who, in some cases, Orwell came to know personally) were Ignazio Silone, an Italian antifascist and later ex-communist novelist whose book-length dialogue on contemporary totalitarian leaders, *The School for Dictators* (1938), Orwell reviewed in June 1939. Among a number of books by Franz Borkenau, an Austrian ex-communist and political scientist who eventually found refuge from the Nazis in England, that Orwell reviewed favorably, the two containing insights relevant to this study are *World Communism: A History of the Communist International* (1938) and *The Totalitarian Enemy* (1940). Because we today have access to an abundance of material on the present and past conditions of life in the Soviet Union, we should not assume that Orwell and his contemporaries had easy access to trustworthy information. The relative scarcity of reliable accounts of Soviet life lends special importance to works on this subject that Orwell did read: Boris Souvarine's booklet *Cauchemar en*

Introduction

U.R.S.S. (Nightmare in the U.S.S.R., 1937) details the ruthless and sometimes absurd Moscow purge trials of the 1920s and 1930s; studded with charts and statistical tables, Nikolai De Basily's encyclopedic *Russia Under Soviet Rule: Twenty Years of Bolshevik Experiment* (1938) records the systematic efforts made to collectivize all aspects of life in the Soviet Union; and an intimate picture of the human, emotional toll exacted by the Revolution—the rage and irrationality and guilt behind the official image of enlightened planning—is provided by American journalist Eugene Lyons's *Assignment in Utopia* (1937). Although the book-length political essays of the American conservative James Burnham are ordinarily regarded as an intellectual source for the bleak vision of unshakable totalitarian control in *Nineteen Eighty-Four*, this study focuses on Burnham's *The Machiavellians, Defenders of Freedom* (1943), an exposition of the ideas of Machiavelli and his modern followers, as contributing a positive note to the tone of *Animal Farm*.

Whereas tracing the novelistic lineage of *Nineteen Eighty-Four* leads from the political fiction of Silone and Arthur Koestler back through the dystopian fantasies of Huxley and Zamiatin and from there to London's *The Iron Heel*, following the spoor of *Animal Farm* leads back to the animal classics of Orwell's and his readers' youth and childhood—Kipling's *Jungle Books* (1894-95) and shorter tales, particularly "A Walking Delegate" (1898), Beatrix Potter's *The Tale of Pigling Bland*, book 4 ("A Voyage to the Houyhnhnms") of *Gulliver's Travels* (1726), and H. G. Wells's *The Island of Doctor Moreau* (1896). Wells's story of the scientist who uses the isolation of a remote island to combine painful surgical procedures with mental conditioning in an ill-conceived attempt to turn captive animals into human beings resonates through *Animal Farm*.

If from these works came images and motifs that buried themselves in the imagination of young Eric Blair to be resurrected years later by George Orwell the novelist, it was from Charles Dickens more than any other imaginative writer that Orwell drew inspiration for a basic strategy of *Animal Farm*. One reason Dickens used more or less literary devices and forms associated with children's literature and expressive of the preadolescent mentality was to free the adult Victorian reader from his prison of acquisitiveness and emotionally impoverishing rationality. During the 1930s sociopolitically committed writers used similar literary types and techniques for very different purposes— to awaken a Dickensian public to political perils too massive to be comprehensible to the Victorian mind. In view of the admiration Orwell revealed in the essay "Charles Dickens" for that writer's ability to re-create a child's fresh and vivid and highly subjective view of reality,[50] it seems likely that in choosing the beast fable form for a mid-twentieth-century novel Orwell wished to include in his narrative a literary element capable of balancing the modern reader's preoccupation with the morally dispiriting realities of twentieth-century politics with animal imagery heavily charged with the saving power of a personal and collective past. Allegorized, the animals in Orwell's fable are politicized beasts of burden, their roles in the narrative tending to reduce them to the level of political functionaries—to turn them into furry or feathered *apparatchiki* (party bureaucrats). Moving centrifugally away from the burning wheel of revolutionary violence and the politicized literary imagination, the creatures and their rustic environment become the embodiment of pastoral wholeness and innocence—a sort of outpost of unprogress in a world of frightening metamorphoses.

Since here Orwell's other writings are also regarded as a source of images and motifs important to an understanding of *Animal Farm*, the following is a thumbnail summary of books with which the reader may not be familiar. *Down and Out in Paris and London* (1933) is a two-part account of Orwell's search for work in Paris, his job as a dishwasher in a plush hotel restaurant, and, in England, his experience of the hardship and squalid living conditions of jobless vagabonds. Hoping to redeem a life wasted on drink and prostitutes in the East, John Flory, the literate and anti-imperialist protagonist of *Burmese Days* (1934), is driven to suicide by a priggish white woman's indifference and the hostility of a native ex-mistress and an ambitious Burmese official. Dorothy Hare, the title character of *A Clergyman's*

Introduction

Daughter (1935), suffers a spell of amnesia connected with an actual or fabricated sexual escapade. After various experiences as a hop picker, London tramp, and teacher in a girl's school, Dorothy returns to her life of workaday drudgery at her father's rural rectory. In *Keep the Aspidistra Flying* (1936), Gordon Comstock, bitter that he is better suited to writing advertisements than poetry, allows himself to sink down the social and economic scale until the pregnancy of his girlfriend motivates a sudden return to the middle-class life of ambition and marital respectability. In different chapters of *The Road to Wigan Pier* (1937), Orwell examines the hard working conditions and substandard domestic circumstances of mining families in the North, sketches the development of his own socialist attitudes, and ridicules middle-class socialist thought based on extensive industrialization. *Homage to Catalonia* (1938) combines an account of Orwell's frontline experiences among the anti-Franco militia with an exposé of the purging in Barcelona of revolutionary factions by Spanish communists allied with the middle class. In *Coming Up for Air* (1939), George Bowling—disgruntled middle-aged and middle-class insurance salesman, husband, and father—takes a sentimental journey to his childhood home of Lower Binfield, and, finding his Edwardian past all but obliterated by modernization, returns to his present home with a mind filled with forebodings about an approaching age of totalitarianism. And as everyone knows, *Nineteen Eighty-Four* (1949) deals with Winston Smith's doomed attempt to enjoy a private life of emotional and physical intimacy in a police state determined to obliterate its subjects' individuality.

Chapter 5 of this study deals with the tension in *Animal Farm* and earlier works between a pastoral condition of existence and the divisive effects of modernization. Chapter 6 describes the development of Orwell's political consciousness and the threat to the pastoral ideal from the emergence of neo-barbaric impulses. Chapter 7 deals with the relationship between Orwell's view of his role as writer and thinker in the 1940s and the formal, tonal, and thematic characteristics of *Animal Farm*.

5

SOME *PER*VERSIONS OF ———
PASTORAL

POLITICS ON THE FARM

Discussing in *Some Versions of Pastoral* various forms of the English
pastoral from the seventeenth century to the twentieth, William Empson, Orwell's friend and colleague at the BBC during the early 1940s,
describes the basic characteristic of the pastoral as the "complex"
made "simple."[51] One of Orwell's main criticisms about the changes
having occurred in England over the last several hundred years, and
particularly during the period of industrialization and urbanization
since the middle of the nineteenth century, is that a reverse process has
taken place. The simple, the life of man in nature, has been made more
complicated. Perhaps it was out of a need to find at least temporary
refuge from the complexities of life in the mid-thirties that in April
1936 Orwell moved into a cottage in the remote Hertfordshire village
of Wallington, south of London—a dwelling that his biographer Bernard Crick terms "ancient" and "*very* simple." Here, in a house with
a detached privy, without electricity, under a corrugated iron roof that
was, Crick says, "abominably noisy" during rains, Orwell and Eileen
Blair, his wife, lived off and on until the 1940s.[52]

Some Perversions of Pastoral

In reference to his subject's fondness for animals, Crick notes Orwell's tendency as an adult to set up "small menageries," usually with the excuse that they would serve a practical function, and at Wallington he kept chickens, geese, and goats, grew vegetables and also cultivated a small orchard.[53] Unlike Farmer Jones in *Animal Farm*, who allows his animals to go unfed, Orwell had a sense of responsibility for the well-being of his domestic animals. In 1938, forced by poor health to leave England for a recuperative stay in Morocco, he arranged for the writer Jack Common to live at the cottage rent free in return for his taking care of the livestock.[54] A letter to Jack Common on 12 October 1938 indicates that Orwell was a man who valued nature over money, for he firmly rejected the temptation to reap a quick and large profit from a soil-exhausting crop.[55] And years after having left Wallington, it is as an advocate of sensible farming that he recalls with marked disapproval a Wallington gamekeeper who, to preserve the overvalued pheasant, routinely destroyed a range of useful predators.[56] Paul Potts, a poet whom Orwell befriended and who visited him on the island of Jura during the later years of his life, calls attention to Orwell's attraction to country life, particularly to the northern Scottish highlands, and to his strong feelings about animals—his great fondness for horses, otters, and hares, and his distaste for cats and rabbits.[57]

Although the writer George Orwell is sometimes called a literary naturalist, a term not ordinarily associated with a sentimental view of nature, there are in his works more than a few traces of an attitude that would justify a designation such as post–late romantic. Some critics have gone so far as to ascribe to Orwell a religious devotion to nature. Along with Thomas Hardy and D. H. Lawrence, Orwell is said to have regarded the natural world as "sacred and sacramental,"[58] as a secular "scripture" supporting his belief in the value of life.[59]

Empson describes three traditionally held views of nature: nature as either itself divine or revelatory of the divine, nature as sympathetic to man and correspondent to the human "social order," and nature as amoral and thus an object of contemplation that offers man "relief" from moral concerns.[60] Orwell's tendency to stress the naturalistic aspects of man and his environment leaves little or no room in his writings for a mystical or recognizably pantheistic vision of the natural world. In different ways the two other views of nature—as a model of human social interaction or as an alternative to it—are important aspects of his works. Certainly Orwell's characters turn to nature, to fields and flowers and trees, as a sanctuary from the emotional and moral stresses of urban life. On the other hand, as will be discussed in chapter 6, the rise of atavistically violent political movements in the twentieth century brought with them the disturbing realization that demagogic appeals to natural impulse unchecked by civilized and civilizing constraints might capture the allegiance of great masses of people.

Writing to Jack Common from Morocco on 26 December 1938, Orwell did not allow his preoccupation with literary and political matters—the possibility that some of his books would be reprinted, the plan to write an "enormous novel" on some "big subject," and outrage at European imperialistic practices—to keep him from remembering his goat, Muriel, whom he asked Common to have suitably mated.[61] However, whatever may have been the caprine destiny awaiting the real goat at Wallington, it appears that the fate of her fictional counterpart in *Animal Farm*, also named Muriel, is closely bound up with a set of circumstances that contribute to the development in her of a disturbing political awareness. As one of the nonporcine beasts both gifted and cursed with an ability to read, even if haltingly, Muriel is the first of the humbler animals to be exposed to the gradual, steady corruption of the language of the revolution. First, in response to the request of the mare Clover, Muriel reads aloud the commandment that has been altered to allow animals—meaning, of course, only the pigs—to sleep in beds, so long as they are sheetless. Later, when Benjamin the donkey refuses a similar request from Clover, Muriel utters the words of an even more serious alteration—the secretly revised commandment allowing for the killing of other animals as long as there is sufficient cause. And it is Muriel who, still unaware that she is in effect announcing the subversion of revolutionary idealism, notes that another human custom, the drinking of alcohol, is allowable (57,

76, 91). The ominous feature of the last-mentioned instance of reading is that the betrayal and power-hunger encoded in the changed wording about alcohol consumption is being internalized by Muriel, who is reading the revised commandment "to herself." It is suggested that this silent reading is a form of inner pollution that devitalizes the animal. Later her faltering attempt to make out the wording on the side of the horse slaughterer's van taking Boxer away is roughly interrupted by Benjamin, and the only subsequent reference to Muriel is the narrator's later remark in passing about her having been dead for an unspecified period of time (91, 101, 106). It is as though the words entering into Muriel's consciousness, and to some extent creating that consciousness, are an intellectual virus that undermines her animal endurance and vitality.

Willing to take the time to "read" the "newspaper" to those farmyard animals that lack her facility with the written word (28), the Muriel who cannot recall the original version of the commandments she reads may be the literary reincarnation of another fictional character who is both literate (with a tutorial bent) and forgetful—Dorothy Hare, the heroine of *A Clergyman's Daughter*. Like Muriel before the painted commandments of *Animal Farm*, the amnesiac Dorothy at one point in the narrative reads the tabloid headlines about her real or imaginary sexual escapades on the Continent without any understanding of their meaning, and later her career as a teacher is effectively aborted by Mrs. Creevy's sudden gag order preventing Dorothy from speaking about controversial subjects to her students (137).

Among the significant natural features of Orwell's landscapes, realistic or symbolic, are hills. In *Burmese Days* it is implied that the psychological and external factors responsible for Flory's eventual destruction are set in operation when he left his isolated timber camp beyond a distant range of "blackish hills" (18) and became involved in the complicated and corrupting life of the colonial station; bracketing the narrative of Dorothy Hare's adventures in London and the south of England is the rise, Knype Hill, atop which she has been raised and to which she returns as a retreat from the mind-numbing complexities of modern England; and in *Nineteen Eighty-Four* hills, ancient seats of power, are symbolic of the state's puritanical assault on human sexuality—the collective power of the massive, pyramidal ministries in opposition to the bodily mound, the *mons veneris,* of the sexually provocative Julia.

In *Animal Farm* it is the knoll on which is charted the course of the narrative. Excited and exhilerated on the first morning of their freedom from human rule and the prospect of meanly rewarded drudgery, the beasts rush up the knoll to survey what has suddenly become their own brave new world—a space that, as predicted by Old Major, is devoid of man and thus "theirs" to enjoy as they wish. Overcome by "ecstasy," the animals for a moment lose control as they jump up, throw themselves into the wet grass, and savor its taste while deeply inhaling the "rich scent" of the soil (18–19).

If this is a brave new world, one in which they are—for now, anyway—no longer the collective embodiment of nature owned, nature under contract to be exploited, abused, and even destroyed for profit, this is also a brave *old* world. Liberated from their ordinary identities as beasts of burden and sources of food, they suddenly become aware of the soil as something that they can experience with an immediate sensory intimacy. For a Dionysiac moment they are experiencing something in danger of being lost to the beasts after thousands of years of domestication—a primal oneness with physical reality. Years before, in *A Clergyman's Daughter,* Dorothy experiences an even briefer moment of rapture in nature when, taking time off from her onerous, physically distasteful parish duties, she allows herself to slip into a "half-pagan ecstasy" in the midst of summer flora and fauna (65). But more bloody than the three pricks from a rose thorn Dorothy administers to herself to regain her Christian sobriety is the circuit taken by the animals back to their servile state, and their knoll is less secure as a refuge from the world's oppressiveness than is Knype Hill. On this knoll is erected by order of the animals' self-seeking leader, Napoleon, the windmill from the ruins of which is conjured up the defeatist myth of the revolution betrayed. To this rise the stunned humbler beasts retreat, their minds and memories filled with the scene of the "slaughter" of fellow beasts offered up to keep the myth of betrayal alive. And it is here that takes place the first scene of the most poignant of the sacrificial rituals marking the transition from revolutionary idealism to dystopian gloom—the collapse of the cruelly overworked cart horse, Boxer (60, 73, 99).

LOSS OF THE PAST

"Horses," Orwell notes in *The Road to Wigan Pier,* "belong to the vanished agricultural past" (201). And Orwell's placement of horses, particularly Boxer, so near the thematic center of *Animal Farm* indicates the importance of the link between nature and the past, both in the personal experience of individuals and the collective experience of English society in general. In choosing to convey his view and vision of contemporary reality by means of the beast fable, a very old literary form not particularly fashionable during the period between the wars, Orwell seems to be calling attention to the value he places on the past. Running through Orwell's writings is the belief that the quality of life was superior to the present in some period prior to either the Boer War or World War I,[62] a conviction expressive of a generalized nostalgia among contemporary Englishmen for the pre-1914 past.[63]

In *Down and Out in Paris and London* one of the more pathetic inhabitants of the Paris working-class quarter where Orwell lived and worked for several months at the end of the 1920s, is Furex, a "strange creature," who, having lost all memory of his life prior to 1914, on weekends drinks himself into a "paroxysm" and while in this condition is hit by a car and killed (93). In light of the importance Orwell attaches to retaining a sense of the past in an age of disorienting and disruptive change, Furex's story may be regarded as symbolic, his ill-starred life an allegorical fable of the perils awaiting those who grow estranged from their origins. This may be one of the reasons why, as T. R. Fyvel, a close friend of Orwell's, has claimed, the setting of *Animal Farm* is a realistically depicted farm in a "timeless Edwardian land-scape."[64]

In *Coming Up for Air* Orwell says that the 1914–18 "war had jerked me out of the old life I'd known, but in the queer period that came afterwards I forgot it almost completely" (145). Implicit in Bowling's observation and lament in *Coming Up for Air* is one of Orwell's main concerns—the problematic relationship between the individual's and the community's present and past. The struggle to overcome forgetfulness, to become aware even of the fact that one has forgotten, and remember the way back to a state of being once known with physical immediacy—this is one of the key motives within Orwell's characters. And this is a longing all the more urgent for those who feel themselves pushed along by the force of circumstances—like the colonial policeman in Orwell's essay "Shooting an Elephant," who feels the native crowd compelling him needlessly to shoot the beast in question—toward an inhospitable future.

Like the unfortunate Furex described in *Down and Out in Paris and London*, Farmer Jones sinks into a state of forgetfulness so extreme as to dissolve his own connection with the soil, his animal possessions, and thus his sense of identity with the past. The opening scene of the novel is that of Jones, coming back to the farm drunk from an evening at the Red Lion inn and making himself even drunker with another glass of beer at home, irresponsibly forgetting to protect his fowls by closing the henhouse popholes, thereby exposing them to potential predators (3). Three months later Jones's stuporous condition, again owing to a pint or two too many at the Red Lion, thrusts him and the whole farm into history when the neglected, desperately hungry animals break into a storage shed containing feed, put Jones and his whip-wielding farm hands to flight, and thus effect a rebellion (17).

Although Orwell's barnyard creatures are affected by Old Major's recital of the various forms of mistreatment and exploitation they have suffered as Farmer Jones's possessions, and for the most part they listen attentively to the boar's prophecy of a happier future without humanity's cruel presence, what brings the animals together in a collective state of the "wildest excitement" is the song "Beasts of England," the complete lyrics of which, claims Old Major, suddenly appeared out of the recent memory of a tune his own mother and other

Some Perversions of Pastoral

sows once sang to their young (10–12). "Supposedly lost to memory for generations" and now rescued from oblivion, "Beasts of England" is for the worker animals, those not caught up in a Gadarene stampede toward the future, a lifeline to the past that makes it possible for them to feel hopeful about the future. Later, the replacement of "Beasts of England" by the official entertainer Minimus's "Animal Farm" marks the crucial change from collective longing for a freer existence to a government-enforced enthusiasm for a utopia officially proclaimed as now achieved (75).

When Orwell discusses British history, the span of time with which he is usually concerned extends to around the middle of the nineteenth century. Even though the Victorian period no more includes all that is good any more than the present is an entirely negative age, for Orwell the evil of the second quarter of the twentieth century is more demoralizing than that of earlier times. Orwell shares the modern view of history as the record of man's expanding consciousness as well as a chronicle of physical achievements. As Orwell sees it, the expansion of consciousness means an increasing awareness of misdeeds that previously would have remained outside consciousness. Orwell sees in the subject of his essay "Rudyard Kipling" (February 1942) a quality, or rather the lack of a quality, that distinguishes the Victorian from the modern—the consciousness of the ethical implications of imperialistic expansionism. Typical of his time, Kipling could not understand that talk about civilizing non-European populations was a cover for economic exploitation or that expansionist enthusiasm was no excuse for brutality and injustice. Such nescience is, however, denied to the twentieth-century imperialist, who knows that the quest for absolute power over others has nothing to do with a civilizing mission. It is this inescapable awareness of wrongdoing that provides the main contrast between the twentieth-century authoritarian political activists and their Victorian predecessors, largely ignorant of the moral implications of their actions.[65]

Determined to prevent their fellow human beings from enjoying life in a "simple and spontaneous way," the Orwellian villain is characterized by a disdain for the past.[66] After his Spanish Civil War experience Orwell became increasingly alarmed at the disrespect shown for historical accuracy by writers more concerned with manipulating public attitudes along ideological lines than with factual truth. In *Animal Farm* the historical past as an independently existing body of facts, the view of history held by Orwell, is turned into an instrument of psychological control by Napoleon in the same way that the puppies he secretly raises are turned into the means of physical terrorism.

Animal Farm chronicles first the dramatically sudden development of a collective consciousness among the animals of Manor Farm, a consciousness based on a common sense of their perilous condition, then, from this group consciousness the idea of progress—the heady expectancy of a future that will be radically different from and somehow more satisfying than the past. And one reason why the reality of the animals' lives after the revolution is at times disappointing and disillusioning is that they have been conditioned to think futuristically, to assume that what the future holds in store must be more appealing than what they have had. What produces the first gathering of animals described in the novel is the expectation of hearing about Old Major's "strange dream," which, he eventually and tersely states, was composed of two aspects—a picture or conception of a world without human beings and the memory of the tune once sung to him and other piglets by their sows. However, worth noting about Old Major's dream is the process by which it is transformed from a glimpse of the past into a marching order directed toward the future. Although the desire to learn about the boar's dream is strong enough in the farm animals to motivate their risking the wrath of Farmer Jones by their clandestine assembly, itself a crypto-rebellion, Old Major no sooner mentions the dream than he waves it aside to make way for a political speech delivered to condition his audience to act. And when Old Major finally gets around to the dream, those aspects that might authenticate its primitiveness—the sows' crooning of a merely fragmentary utterance ("they knew only the tune and the first three words") and the ancestral memory of a zoological period before the appearance of *homo sapiens*—become the components of an activist, future-oriented program. The earth devoid of human beings is a condition that "will" be actualized, presumably after humanity has been exterminated; Old Major is dogmatically "certain" that he knows the whole song of which he heard only three words in his infancy; and in inducing the animals to memorize and sing the lyrics of "Beasts of England" he is in effect conditioning them to accept the authoritarian dictates of his porcine successors (10–11). We may be justified in suspecting that Old Major's secret intention of using his dream to indoctrinate the other animals for the future has led him to falsify the fragmentary nature of the original dream by imposing on it a form of certitude designed to reinforce the ideological content of his speech.

Events and circumstances both within and outside of Manor/Animal Farm conspire to instill into the animals' budding consciousness not only a distrust and possibly an abhorrence of a specific aspect of the past—their sufferings under Farmer Jones—but also an indifference to the past in itself. Those moments during the early stage of the revolution when the animals revel in the newly discovered delight of freedom and thrill to the words proclaiming universal animal equality remain just that—moments that fade away in the creatures' conscious minds as they are herded into the future. Although the erosion of the postrevolutionary beasts' original enthusiastic idealism is due in part to particular acts of greed or distrust or malevolence, what gives a tragic undertone to the melodrama of evil and innocence is the circumstance that history itself is exerting its impersonal power to force leaders and followers alike down a road taking them farther from the concrete and limited goals for which they struggled so bravely toward a shapeless future.

A CLOSER LOOK AT FARMER JONES

In view of the widening gap between the predictions and proclamations about the quality of life on the postrevolutionary farm made by the porcine intellectuals (Old Major, Snowball, Squealer) and the humbler animals' felt experience of farm life, a reader should be careful not to accept statements of dubious authority without criticism.

Indeed, certain reactions to statements made by Orwell himself suggest that raising a few vegetables and tending a handful of animals now and then did not make that city intellectual an expert on either farming or animal psychology. In order to develop a thesis about the evils of colonialism, Orwell begins a section in "Marrakech" with the scene of a gazelle he has just fed butting him away for fear of becoming his prey[67]—Orwell's intention being to suggest a parallel between man's carnivoracity and colonial exploitation. Some years later, intent on contrasting the self-conscious urban nature lover with the farmer's unthinking and untutored closeness to nature, Orwell attributes to the latter an easy acceptance of inaccurate folk beliefs about animals.[68] However, one critic's response to Orwell's encounter with the gazelle was another butting—the charge that were Orwell's outlook not so habitually negative he might have recognized the gazelle's action as a normal feeding response.[69] And a letter appearing in the *Manchester Evening News* a week after Orwell's remark on farmers' reassuring misconceptions charged him with having a "very limited" knowledge of the subject.[70]

The apparent gaps in the urbanite Orwell's knowledge of things rustic and zoological suggests the wisdom of the Lower Binfield boys, as they are recollected by the first-person narrator of *Coming Up for Air*, in allowing into their gang several "farm lads" who know "twice as much about animals" as did the town youths (65). This in turn suggests that an investigation into the factors responsible for the deteriorating conditions on prerevolutionary Manor Farm should start with the farmer himself—Jones. It is worth noting that even before the animal uprising that dispossesses him and accelerates his self-destructive alcoholism, he is a hapless, defeated man—a man marked for ruin. Sociologically, he seems representative of the small landholder described in a book reviewed by Orwell in May 1936, Alec Brown's *The Fate of the Middle Classes*, whom the expansionist imperatives of "monopoly capitalism" were allegedly pushing off the land in the 1930s. Moreover, some parallels between Jones and earlier Orwellian characters suggest a link between his misfortunes and problems and dilemmas and those described in Orwell's more realistic narratives. The cause-effect relationship between the nocturnal theft of money from Orwell's Paris hotel and his change of identity from middle-class writer in the making to lower-class kitchen worker, as described in *Down and Out in Paris and London,* bears some resemblance to the loss of money through a lawsuit and the actual or imagined nocturnal predation by a fox that precede Jones's decline from farmer to propertyless barfly in *Animal Farm.* And the buckshot from his gun that hits nothing but the barn wall (12) reminds us of an earlier off-the-mark shot fired by another man on the road to ruin—Flory in *Burmese Days*—at another canine, a pariah dog howling at the moon outside his house (73).

The relationship between *Animal Farm* and Orwell's earlier works may become clearer if we take a leaf from Peter Stansky and William Abraham's biography, *The Unknown Orwell*[71]—specifically, the title page—and start work on "the unknown Farmer Jones," the subject of which has, under various names and identities, a checkered career through the thirties prior to his appearance as owner of Manor Farm. So beguiling is Orwell's presentation of the animal characters in *Animal Farm* that Jones has received relatively little notice, usually being viewed as little more than a two-dimensional emblem of proprietorial callousness or as a cartoon depiction of the deposed Russian Czar Nicholas II. Like Elizabeth Lackersteen in *Burmese Days* with Flory after his inglorious fall from a polo pony—"she . . . looked at him and through him as though he had not existed" (188)—the reader educated in the ways of allegorical interpretation tends to look through Jones the fictionally realistic character and focus on Jones the political concept or Jones the somebody else. There is, however, more to this character than is immediately apparent, and a closer look reveals depths and ambiguities that indicate a kinship between him and other Orwellian figures whose deterioration follows their loss of a past intimacy with nature.

In the essay "The Art of Donald McGill" (1941), Orwell describes the English comic postcard as offering an "unheroic" view of man—a comically reductive picture of the "unredeemed lowness" of ordinary life, of a world populated by characters whose behavior answers to the stereotyped expectations of the people who buy these cards. One commonplace stereotype is that of the "red-nosed" husband drunkenly returning home in the small hours of the morning while an angry wife is shown waiting "behind the front door, poker in hand."[72] Reeling across the farmyard and downing the last of many glasses of beer before hazarding the stairs to bed—at first sight Farmer Jones looks as though he himself has stepped out of a comic postcard. However, for various reasons his behavior hints at ambiguities beyond the two-dimensional crudity of the cartoon. Why, we might ask, would a farmer worried enough about predators to keep a gun in his bedroom allow his hens to be endangered through the night by forgetting to close the passageways into the henhouse, a piece of carelessness made more puzzling by the caution he displays in kicking off his boots before entering the house? And how likely is it that he could effectively deal with a predator after an extra glass of beer on arriving home? One answer is that there is more than one Jones. Perhaps revealed by the late-night hour and the alcohol is a self not apparent in the daylight Jones. In some way linked to the men of violence behind the "machine guns squirting out of bedroom windows" that George Bowling envisions in Coming Up for Air (267), Jones may have drunk himself into forgetfulness with the unconscious intention of making a barnyard disturbance more likely and thus giving him an excuse to fire his weapon—a Macbeth murdering sleep—to proclaim his power over nature. Yet the shooting is symbolically the negation of Jones's dominance: hitting the barn, he is destroying his own property, denying the value of his own accomplishments, and it is as though with the shotgun pellets he is designating the place for the revolutionary laws that will formally confirm his eventual dispossession and exile.

There is yet another Jones in the drunken figure lurching up the stairs to bed, an alter ego to the angry, destructive, and even self-destructive man later to fire out the bedroom window. In the "Trafalgar Square" passage in A Clergyman's Daughter, a Joycean dialogue by tramps trying to live through a freezing winter night, Dorothy hears a Mrs. McElligot's anecdote about the time when she and a male companion survived a similar night in a pigsty: "So in we goes, an' dere was an old sow lay on his side snorin' . . . I creeps up agen her an' puts me arms round her, an' begod she kept me warm all night" (179). What gives this story a special significance in regard to Dorothy Hare is that during the course of the narrative, events have very nearly driven her into the hyperconscious condition of the post-Kipling urbanite inescapably and painfully aware of modern society's exploitative character. From the very start of the novel Dorothy is Gissing's odd woman out: with their "antiphonal snoring" the Reverend Hare and (presumably in another room) the maid sleep the sleep of the socially unaware, but for the protagonist it seems that there can be no such refuge—"Come on, Dorothy," she exhorts herself, "up you get! No snoozing, please!" (5). It may well be a primitive need to escape into the peace of an animal slumber, deep and undisturbed by the complexities of the adult individual's waking existence, that accounts for Jones's final glass of beer before being enclosed in the warmth of his own sow, the "snoring" Mrs. Jones (3).

However, the "large bottle" of medicine that the pigs find in the Joneses' bathroom (100) suggests something less than a condition of animal health in one or both of the spouses, and the fact that while in the conjugal bed Jones needs the assurance of his phallic, ever-erect gun, "which always [stands] in a corner of his bedroom" (12), raises more questions about the nature of the marriage itself. At one point in *Keep the Aspidistra Flying*, Gordon Comstock, his alcoholically offensive sexual advances having been rebuffed by his girlfriend, becomes even more inebriated and then goes to a brothel. By now, however, he is impotent: "No use. Impossible. . . . The booze, it must be. See Macbeth" (176). Even if both Farmer Jones and his wife lack Comstock's bookish foreknowledge regarding the way in which alcohol "takes away the performance" of "lechery"—to use the words of the porter in *Macbeth*—experience has surely taught them what not to expect after the husband's evening of steady drinking at the Red

Lion. And for reasons that should become clear later in this chapter and elsewhere, the "pink medicine" in the cabinet may take the place of drinks at the pub in rendering the wife oblivious to her husband's physical presence.

What is suggested by the opening chapter of *Animal Farm* is man's alienation from nature not only as external reality but also in the form of his primal instincts and drives. Although the narrative does not give enough information to infer the specific factors responsible for Farmer Jones's uneasiness in the bedroom, a partial explanation may be suggested by a passage in one of Orwell's unpublished literary notebooks—a male's thoughts about women, presumably intended for use in a planned but unwritten fictional work. Marriage reveals "two great facts ab[out] women," one being their "incorrigible dirtiness and untidiness," the other, and more disturbing, conclusion being about women's "terrible, devouring sexuality." Because the woman, the wife, is "quite insatiable" and seemingly "never . . . fatigued f[rom] no matter how much love-making," after a year conjugal intimacy becomes for the male a "duty, a service."[73]

To perceive the contrast between animal closeness and human estrangement in *Animal Farm* more clearly, we might trace the prehistory of the "silk dress" that Jones's wife would ordinarily wear to Sunday service and that eventually graces the ample proportions of Napoleon's "favorite sow" (113). At a certain distance the dried leaves beneath the "phallic" trees among which Gordon Comstock and Rosemary, in *Keep the Aspidistra Flying*, search for a spot to make love look like "folds of copper-coloured silk" (126). To George Bowling on the road back to Lower Binfield in *Coming Up for Air*, the "silky-looking" field of wheat he passes is "like a woman," on which he would like to "lie" (203–4). Suggesting the diminished quality of life in the Joneses' marriage is the fact that the human wife's silk dress has been reserved for Sunday wear, the sensual ambience of its fabric suppressed beneath the weight of Sabbath decorum, whereas the new owner is only one of a number of sows whose many piglets (94) attest to Napoleon's sexual activity. It may be added that the Jones marriage gives even less evidence of issue than does the apparently childless union of Lord and Lady Macbeth.

In Kipling's somewhat heavy-handed antisocialist beast fable "A Walking Delegate" there occurs a dialogue involving two mares, Miss Tedda and Tuck, and Tuck's brother, Nip. Discussing the pleasures and aggravations of her working life, Tedda hesitantly admits that her male owner once kissed her, and when Tuck marvels at the boldness of some human males, Nip quickly reveals that his sister's shock is all show: "*You* git a kiss reg'lar's hitchin'-up time" (52). In *Burmese Days* appears a character whose ardor for his mare is far more intense than that of Kipling's males. Disgusted with Burma and the Burmans as well as with the white colonials he feels have sunk to the moral level of the natives, abhorring women even when he occasionally succumbs to a physical need for them—Verrall, the military policeman for whom Elizabeth Lackersteen jilts Flory and by whom she is jilted in turn, cares for only one female—the mare he tends with religious veneration and sits astride as though fused with her in a centaurlike union (203). The opening chapter of *Animal Farm* suggests that alongside the ruthlessly utilitarian Farmer Jones of Old Major's diatribe there exists another Jones. This one is best known to Mollie, who pulls his carriage, and is hinted at by the colorfully beribboned mane to which she coyly calls attention during the boar's speech. That Jones has actually switched his affections from human spouse to an attractive equine is indicated by the fact that as soon as Mrs. Jones flees, during the ouster of her husband, Mollie knows just where to go to find more ribbons— to Mrs. Jones's dressing table (19). That these gifts betoken the unformulated longing of a man increasingly alienated from the soil to regain a lost harmony with nature—to regain it with all the mythic intimacy and intensity that the archetypal dream of man-animal unity might promise—is remotely suggested by the Anti-Sex League sash worn by Julia in *Nineteen Eighty-Four* (11), which in fact marks her as the exclusive sexual property of the Inner Party.

In Kipling's story the pastured horses show loyalty to their human masters by mocking the efforts of an equine union organizer to set horses against men, and in *Burmese Days* the centaur gallops out of the station and out of the narrative with mare and man still as one. But times change, and between *Burmese Days* and *Animal Farm* something has happened to separate man from horse, humanity from nature. Something has caused a dissociation of the pastoral sensibility, and if the antiliterary Verrall had ever deigned to read T. S. Eliot, the philistine might have known what hit him when, somewhere between Burma and the England of *A Clergyman's Daughter,* he and his beloved mare parted company. The first object that appears in the new world dawning in the consciousness of Dorothy Hare, a riderless draft horse, is her introduction to a new, fragmented world of urban England, with its "difference . . . between human beings and horses . . . and between men and women" (97).

THE PASTORAL IMAGINATION

In *A Clergyman's Daughter* Orwell may be testing the viability of the pastoral vision of reality in twentieth-century society and in the twentieth-century novel. A criticism made of Orwell's works is that the documentary impulse to focus on certain limited settings and situations—in this case the Kentish hop fields where Dorothy Hare works for a while as a picker, then her experiences as a vagabond in London, and finally her brief tenure at Mrs. Creevy's London school for girls—interferes with the forward movement of the narrative and thus with the development of character in the fiction and line of argument in the nonfiction.[74] Akin to a type of gratuitous detail that—as he indicates in "Charles Dickens" and "Why I Write"—he finds appealing,[75] such more or less fixed, static scenes, vignettes, and episodes in *A Clergyman's Daughter* and elsewhere in Orwell often embody a pastoral element that slows down the forward movement of the realistic narrative. In *Nineteen Eighty-Four,* O'Brien, speaking as an official of the ruling Inner Party, promises the captured rebel Winston Smith that at the end of his ideological reeducation he will be "lifted clean out from the

stream of history" (257). In earlier works O'Brien's promise is anticipated by short or extended passages that are or seem meant to be so
captivating as to lift character and reader out of or dam the flow of
narrative and historical time. Such scenes are pastoral in at least two
different ways: their content—human types, flora and fauna, and
other features associated with rustic life—may be traditionally linked
to the pastoral as a more or less well-defined literary genre or a more
general celebration of the simple life; and the structure may itself exhibit a stylized simplicity that reflects basic patterns underlying the
surface complexity of phenomenal reality, whether rural or urban. As
viewed one evening by the animals from the distanced perspective of
the knoll, Manor Farm is a literary or pictorial "prospect" of bucolic
charm, yet at the same time the persistent afterimage of the bloody
purge having just taken place (71–73) historicizes the fixed, self-contained pictorial scene into the long march of modern social and political change.

In terms of modern experience, the traditional pastoral opposition between the innocence and spontaneity of rustic life and the cun-
ning artificiality of life at court and in the city can take the form of
the individual's private, seemingly timeless states of being that contrast
with an awareness of historical time sharpened on the flint of social
and political activism. Examples of the former condition, of moments
of absorption into nature, are numerous enough to check a common
tendency to regard Orwell as simply a political writer. If in *Burmese
Days* the central character is presented as perfervid critic of the colonial system, he is also solitary acolyte in the temple of nature, his senses
worshipfully attentive to the "great green dome"of a jungle tree alive
with the sounds of invisible birds (57); so narrowed is the thinking of
A Clergyman's Daughter's Dorothy Hare working in a Kentish hop
field that linear time, her life as once experienced in terms of "either
yesterday or to-morrow," ceases to have any meaning for her (135);
and in *Homage to Catalonia* the eagles calmly floating high above the
battle lines, not deigning to notice the shots aimed at them by the
soldiers below (25), seem to belong to another, heraldic reality.

These static elements, the scenes in which the attention is absorbed by and into an object or activity, check for a time the forward motion toward a conclusion, and this tension between stasis and movement reflects a thematic conflict between a sociopolitical impulse, a need to become involved some way with the processes of history, and a counterimpulse toward another mode of existence. Moreover, the central characters in Orwell's narratives, whether fictional or autobiographical, harbor a longing to escape from situations in which their minds as well as bodies are subject to externally imposed authoritarian expectations. Feeling himself forced by the circumstances of station life outwardly to accept a colonial system he finds oppressive and morally corrupting, Flory in *Burmese Days* yearns to become a part of the apparently age-old patterns of native Burma, as is symbolically exhibited in the Burmese girl's ritualized *pwe*-dance (105). In the novel of Orwell's that is most Wellsian in its nostalgia for boyhood, *Coming Up for Air,* the central character's journey to his own hometown is an attempt to transform his present experience of time, an accelerated motion toward a politically violent future, into his boyhood sense of existing in a never-ending present (86).

Sometimes the term "pastoral" is used to designate a class of nineteenth- and twentieth-century novels the action of which, including the development of the characterization, involves a counterpointing of two antithetical modes of life. On the one hand, described in a prose often touched by poetry, is the traditional, premodern world of a relatively static agricultural civilization, its values and patterns of behavior in harmony with the land and the seasons, and impinging on it are the more realistically rendered images of modern commercialized and industrialized society. Thus pastoral may be used as a descriptive term for novels in which the institutions, values, behavior, and even ways of thinking and feeling associated with a life lived close to the green world of nature are played off against those of town and city. Although Orwell's novels of the 1930s fit into this classification, as do nonfictional narratives such as *Homage to Catalonia*, in this study it is more convenient to restrict the term pastoral to the former—both the natural world into which the Orwellian character is drawn and the life-affirming impulses he hopes to awaken within his psyche. The polarities emphasized here in regard to *Animal Farm* are the pastoral and its opposite, the political. Insofar as Orwell's narratives are classifiable as examples of social (although not socialist) realism with their focus on characters positioned near the base of the British social pyramid, they bear some resemblance to Empson's category of "Covert Pastoral," a form of "proletarian art," which he broadly defined as literature "about the people" (presumably the working classes) but not necessarily written by a member of this group or meant to be read by the lower classes.[76] To the extent that Orwell's works bear the stamp of such modernist writers admired by him as T. S. Eliot, E. M. Forster, and D. H. Lawrence, the pastoral element may be an instinctive vitality and spontaneity of which the conscious self may become intuitively aware and with which it feels a more or less urgent need to come into contact.

Perhaps influencing the choice of the initial word in the title of Orwell's *Down and Out in Paris and London* was the tendency in the accounts of earlier sociological explorers to describe their entry into the London slums and working-class districts with metaphors of descent, the best known example of this being Jack London's record of his days in London's East End, *The People of the Abyss* (1904).[77] Downward goes Orwell the kitchen worker in a Paris hotel, into a subterranean "cellar below a cellar," and, as a tramp in London entering a transients' shelter, down into a "cellar deep underground" (*Down and Out in Paris and London*, 133). But whatever the specific motivation for this or that descent, the general pattern suggests a quest for modern urbanized man's buried life—for the natural man, man living and working as intimately and harmoniously with nature as the conditions of twentieth-century life allow. If Flory's river passage from the besieged European Club to a police outpost marks him as the stock hero of the East-of-Suez adventure novel, the downward movement of his adventure—the leap from the Club verandah, the sinking into the river ooze, and the floating downriver to the police compound—carries the white community's savior into the middle of a mass of Burmans, a dreamlike scene in which he, suddenly passive, is absorbed into but not hurt by the collective power of the natives (*Burmese Days*, 250–52). Let the middle-class Bloomsbury intellectual find his art in a book, atop a pedestal, or up the slopes of the Acropolis; but Orwell will go deep underground to admire the "grimy caryatid," the coal miner, on whose bent but sturdy shoulders rests civilization itself (*The Road to Wigan Pier*, 21). Orwell's descent down the mine shaft is a boy's adventure to the center of the earth, a return to some primeval womb, a search for bedrock reality. So far down is Orwell's trip into the coal miner's workaday environment that he seems to go below the origin of organic life itself: for above him are the "bones of extinct beasts, subsoil, flints, roots of growing things, green grass and cows grazing on it" (*The Road to Wigan Pier*, 24).

Implicit in these descents is the belief that in twentieth-century England natural man is submodern, subcapitalist, and subbourgeois. He, or rather they—since the relative closeness to nature is, in Orwell, usually a group condition—can be found among Asian natives, English tramps, and Kentish hop-pickers, many of whom are Gypsies proudly unassimilated into contemporary society.[78] Orwell's natural man is, therefore, not a grown-up wild child, a primitive, or *l'homme sauvage* of the eighteenth-century philosophers living apart from modern civilization, but rather a person with a social identity, usually on the margin of contemporary urban civilization.

One of the most important aims of Orwell's earlier works is to measure the extent to which an individual burdened by modern civilization and its discontents might be able to reclaim some remnant of a vanishing heritage. The town of Knype Hill, the first setting described in *A Clergyman's Daughter*, is a microcosmic London at the center of a surrounding region that—"ancient, agricultural and respectable" to the south, and with a factory area to the north—mimics modern England as a whole (16–17). We are to see Dorothy Hare as a representative of the twentieth-century Englishman being pushed forward by the pressure of events and circumstances into the urban and industrial future. Paradoxically, the amnesia that suppresses the memory of her contemporary identity as rectory drudge obsessed with the unpaid bills piling up because of her father's financial irresponsibility allows her to remember back to England's agricultural past. This remembering back is physical, not mental, and takes the form of Dorothy's almost mindless trek to the hop fields of Kent, to southern feudal England.

Her guide to the rough-cut pastoral existence as a field laborer is a curious creature, Nobby, who will appear both later and earlier in *Coming Up for Air,* on a World War I battlefield. "She'd do jest nicely for Nobby," someone says in reference to Dorothy in *A Clergyman's Daughter*, and it does appear that Nobby bears the credentials needed to bring out the woman's latent responsiveness to nature. Even on cold nights able to sleep "peacefully" on the bare ground, guiltlessly gathering nature's abundance as fruits and vegetables even when it is private property, and unable to arrange his "picturesque memories" into a "consecutive account of his life" (100, 108–9, 113)—he looks very much like an authentic pastoral type. References to his simian facial features and his hooflike foot (100–1, 109, 112) add to this impression, suggesting a creature on the threshold between humanity and animality.

At one point in Cervantes's *Don Quixote* the famous knight-errant falls asleep in the cavern of Montesinos, and after dreaming that he is in a place where for centuries lords and ladies have been kept preserved under an enchantment by Merlin, he has a vision of three peasant girls disporting themselves in a meadow like frolicsome goats. "In a dreamlike state" (119), the Dorothy of the Kentish hop fields is a modern version of the Spaniard. On the one hand, the Kent section of *A Clergyman's Daughter* is a realistic documentary intended to dispel any falsely romantic views of agricultural life the urban reader might entertain: Charlie and Flo, the cockneys accompanying Nobby and Dorothy on the road south, soon get their fill of country hardships and return to London, and only the first night Dorothy spends in a pile of drafty and prickly straw is not a torment to her (118, 130). On the other hand, in its own way the Kent episode is a vision of a past condition of natural contentment and goodness, one foreshadowing the dream that restores to the dying Old Major a fragment of his own suckling past. During the day the pickers are sweated wage slaves forced by physical need into an economic identity as functional units within the capitalist system of private ownership of the land and exploitation of it for profit. But at night the pickers become the collective embodiment of an earlier form of society. With the men out raiding orchards or henhouses (taking advantage of any lapses in security on the farms of local Farmer Joneses), the women gathering firewood for the meals, and both together singing or telling stories around a roaring campfire (128–36)—what Dorothy has dreamed herself back to is a primitive hunting and gathering society, a tribe whose members are something like an extended family bound together by a spontaneous sense of communal responsibility and solicitude, not divided by the distrust and competitiveness and acquisitive individualism of the city a few miles to the north. Externally exploited, internally the hop pickers, "very few" of whom have "more than a dim idea" of their earnings (132), are barely if at all touched by the money-consciousness that has soured Dorothy's past existence at Knype Hill and is continuing to do so to the urban wage slaves of contemporary England.

The pure pastoral, the golden age of spontaneous goodness and communal harmony with the rhythms of nature, can maintain itself only in isolation from the city. For Dorothy the grimy, sweat-stained pastoral of the Kentish hop-field life begins collapsing with the appearance in the picker's camp of the policemen who arrest Nobby and his young accomplice (138–39). Besides the isolated and enclosed country setting, there is another type of pastoral, a pastoral condition of being, that is now violated. The word "pastoral" begins with "past," and one reason why Dorothy is so contented in Kent is that through amnesia and the primitive utopianism of the hop-picking community she is able to discard her normal adult existence as the lonely companion—in effect, servant—of an emotionally frigid father in a motherless household and become as a child in a caring communal family. For the adult-turned-child the surest sign that the torn out pages of his or her inner calendar have been restored is when they become the pages of a child's storybook wherein the transformed individual can find compensations for the disappointments of adult life and a means of de-clawing its emotional and physical perils. For two reasons Nobby's presence betokens Dorothy's reentry into childhood: he talks and he does not seduce. The adult Dorothy living in town has lost touch with her childhood—that time when animals and human children have a common language and can communicate as equals— because sexual anxiety blocks the road back. What the reader is supposed to regard as Dorothy's sexual neurosis has taken control of the imagery of childhood, so that in her mind fear of the sexually aroused male takes the form of a "large furry beast" (92). At the opposite extreme is the aloof father, a man lost in his own dreams of the past, who routinely ignores his daughter (36). Nobby is the very reverse of silent father and libidinal beast. Always either singing or recounting bits and pieces of his past, Nobby is as orally vigorous as he is genitally docile, one repulse from Dorothy sufficing to suppress any signs of his hormonal rebelliousness.

But Dorothy's amnesia-induced fragmentation into two selves— hinted at on the first page of the novel by the Prufrockian habit of referring to herself as "you"—may signify not a return to pastoral simplicity but an inescapable vulnerability to an antipastoral complexity and devitalization. The alcoholic apathy that robs Farmer Jones of the will to tend his animals and crops is foreshadowed by the Reverend Hare's distaste for the ancient concerns of his rural parishioners: "The Rector [has] . . . a perfect abhorrence of Harvest Festivals" (27). The counterpart of the clergyman's alienation from the life-giving agricultural rituals of his environment is his daughter's alienation from the life-giving sexuality that may be lying just below the surface of her carefully controlled daily life—a passionateness ready to burst forth into the "half-pagan ecstasy" evoked by the scent of wild flowers or, like the old parishioner's rug she touches, into dozens of cats (65, 68). The dirt-smudged Dorothy standing on a London street some time after her mysterious disappearance from the rectory certainly exhibits one of the traits attributed to women in the passage from Orwell's literary notebook cited earlier in this chapter. And even though the "laddered" state of her "silk stockings" hints at the other trait, that of sexual eagerness, the fact that the silk is "artificial" (98) suggests a woman separated from her own primal naturalness. In "Hop-picking" (1931) Orwell refers the reader to James G. Frazer's *The Golden Bough* as a possible source of information regarding the harvest custom of putting women in the hop bins at the end of the day.[79] Explained by Frazer as a fertility ritual using a female doll or puppet,[80] the practice as described in *A Clergyman's Daughter* seems to be mainly an opportunity for the males to rough up the camp females; and the fact that it is a "butcher-boy" who grips Dorothy during a ring dance around a bonfire seems to counteract the life-giving efficacy of this ritual, described in *The Golden Bough* as a guarantee of the participating maiden's approaching marriage and motherhood.[81]

The sexual uneasiness and generally problematic relationship between men and women in *A Clergyman's Daughter,* and in the other novels as well, cast a long shadow across the stylized landscape of *Animal Farm.* The shotgun blast from Farmer Jones's bedroom is the negation of a life-affirming passionateness, a suppression of the farm beasts' collective display of the "wildest excitement" (12). Dorothy deserts the Reverend Hare in the middle of her work on pasteboard boots for the pageant portrayal of, among other historical figures, Oliver Cromwell, England's most famous revolutionary (95, 313), and with a similar abruptness Mrs. Jones exits during the farm animals' uprising in *Animal Farm* (17). Orwell's refusal to inform the reader as to whether or not Dorothy really did run off with Warburton, a rakish neighbor in the habit of making advances to her, is matched by the news blackout regarding Mrs. Jones's whereabouts after her escape. If, as seems probable, the latter's flight is also a spousal abandonment, it would only ratify a situation in existence from the first—a husband using alcohol to avoid the performance of conjugal rites and a wife whose snoring tolls the end of sensual expectancy. The wintry London scene in which Dorothy wraps herself in newspapers to get some sleep (194) later takes the form of Jones's covering himself with the *News of the World* to nap in peace in *Animal Farm* (16)—the gestures in both cases signifying withdrawal from the complexities of the present into the pastoral calm of slumber. Extending the parallel suggests that the farmer's attachment to Mollie springs less from the adult male's frustrated sexuality than from a more primitive need to reclaim the child's sense of identity with the animal. The pathos of Jones's career is the abyss of silence, of incommunicativeness, between man the owner and his animal possessions, Mollie and the others, except for the unreliable raven, Moses.

MONEY AND MODERN MAN

The closest that Jones can come to sharing the storybook reality of the child and the animal are those few moments when he displays a faint kinship with Mr. McGregor, the chronically irritated gardener in Beatrix Potter's *Peter Rabbit* tales. But when the animals' initially spontaneous revolt against Jones's un-McGregor-like negligence takes the ideological direction mapped out earlier by Old Major's speech, the familiar English Jones becomes Russianized into *kulak* Jones condemned to extinction in the merciless people's court of revolutionary history. However, even before this change Jones has revealed his identity as economic man, for whom nature is valuable only as property, as a collection of functional units organized for production and profit. Ironically, economics turns on Jones even before the animals do: having lost money in a lawsuit, the landowner sinks into a Chekhovian funk, drinking too much and allowing the farm to run down as the farmhands become less and less dependable (16).

"The awful thralldom of money is upon everyone,"[82] Orwell lamented six months before his arrival in revolutionary Barcelona, and several years earlier, in *Down and Out in Paris and London*, he claimed that the main reason why tramps, the great army of the unemployed moving from town to town in the 1930s, are so "despised" is that they have failed the "grand test of virtue" in bourgeois England—to earn a lot of money (174). Money, the pursuit of it and anguish at its lack, is an insistent motif in Orwell's early narratives. In *Down and Out in Paris and London* Orwell emphasizes the physical discomforts of poverty; in *A Clergyman's Daughter* the focus is on money matters as invading the mind and spirit. "At all hours of the night or day [the overdue butcher's bill] was waiting just round the corner of [Dorothy Hare's] consciousness, ready to spring upon her" (8). The spreading obsession with lucre is shown to be subverting institutions traditionally responsible for the nation's spiritual and cultural health, the church and the school. The "fall" that the Reverend Hare broods over is the "drop" in the value of his stocks, and his "lifelong search," is not for a heavenly reward but for a profitable investment (32–33). The list of individuals and their capabilities with which Dorothy is presented during her orientation to Mrs. Creevy's girls' school is not that of the pupils but of the parents, who are graded by the frequency of their payments (222). For modern commercialized man money is a vitamin: with it, he feels healthy and bullish about life, but without it—or with not enough—he is prey to apathy and listlessness. Too ready to excuse his indolence as appropriate for the impoverished descendant of an aristocratic house, the Reverend Hare breezily dismisses the plea of a "common bricklayer" that the clergyman hurry to baptize the workingman's dying infant (29). Similarly, in *Animal Farm* Farmer Jones is so overcome with lethargy after the financial setback of the lost lawsuit that he loses interest in the technical books, including *Every Man His Own Bricklayer* (42), that inspire Snowball's blueprint for the revolutionary future.

The laying of bricks by the worker animals in constructing the windmill does not, however, release them from the thrall of money, for the mounting cost of the structure necessitates a return to cash-crop agriculture (54). If the loss of real money starts Jones on his downward course, an abundance of false money—the fake bank notes proudly displayed by the duped Napoleon to demonstrate an illusory business canniness (84)—reveal the supposedly all-wise leader's trotters of clay. As durable here as any cult of the *führer* and probably more durable than ideological dogma is the cult of cash, money worship. It is the genial deity Lucre whose power is displayed during the dishonest card game that marks the last stage of the farm ruler's decline from porcine dignity to piggish improbity.

Moreover, there may be a connection between the pointed snoring with which Mrs. Jones greets the returning husband and his financial decline, and it seems likely that Jones's pampering of Mollie is responsible for her inability or unwillingness to tolerate the austerities of postrevolutionary farm life and her flight to the *dolce vita* of stroking and sugar cubes offered by a new human owner (40). A characteristic of Orwell's fiction for which he has been criticized, his portrayal of women as primarily biological creatures with only a limited awareness of matters beyond the scope of their immediate needs,[83] is one aspect of Orwell's larger picture of a commercialized civilization the men and women of which have lost contact with their agricultural past and are no longer conscious of a pastoral vitality, spontaneity, and empathy within themselves. A connection between animality and the human female is clearly implied by the memory of a personal fantasy or mental scene recorded in "Why I Write"—that of a male who approaches a window from which he could see a cat playing in the street below. But between the man and the feline are closed curtains of "muslin"[84]—in British English a slang term for woman. The literary significance of this juxtaposition of images is underscored by the fact that in the essay Orwell makes a connection between this recollected mental scene and his early thoughts about a writing career. In Orwell's fiction of the 1930s the animal qualities of the female are emphasized in order to throw into higher relief the emotionally and morally constricting effects of money-consciousness. Having used bribery to rid himself of the Burmese mistress, Ma Hla May, whom he wishes to replace with an English wife, Flory of *Burmese Days* is dismayed to discover that the once kittenish native has become a whitish-hued harridan screaming for more and more money (197). Women, naturally white, the middle-class females of bourgeois-capitalist England, make no attempt to conceal their distaste for nonaffluent males: the only response that a scruffy Gordon Comstock has come to expect from the crowds of women passing him by on the sidewalks of London is coldly indifferent stares. And refreshed from her "animal" slumber, Hermione Slater of *Keep the Aspidistra Flying* uses her sexual power over Ravelston, Gordon's wealthy and guilt-burdened socialist friend, to prevent him from giving money to the poor (72, 93, 99). The half-crown that Dorothy Hare takes from her pocket and displays to the awed Nobby prior to the journey to Kent is a mark of Cain preventing her permanent return to a pastoral condition of simplicity and wholeness, and in the moment that Nobby slips the coin into his own pocket, he sets in motion a process that will turn the natural man's innocent pilfering into a morally dangerous acquisitiveness (*A Clergyman's Daughter*, 101, 104, 138–39).

UTOPIA VERSUS THE HORSE

Toward the end of *A Clergyman's Daughter*, as Warburton accompanies Dorothy on a train back to Knype Hill, the latter notes without comment a "slummy wilderness" stretching out from London—"labyrinths of little dingy-coloured houses . . . great chaotic factories . . . miry canals and derelict building lots littered with rusty boilers and overgrown by smoke-blackened weeds" (292). What she is seeing is a sign of the times—the expansion of an urban bleakness not only over the physical landscape but also across the imaginative landscape of the 1930s, with the great city's monotonous industrial suburbs a symbol of the decade itself. For a writer like Graham Greene this type of setting might be appropriate for the expression of a bleak, soured urban romanticism, but for Orwell bleak is bleak. Orwell's Sheffield, with its "mean little houses blackened" by smoke from innumerable factory chimneys, is "one of the most appalling places" he has ever seen. Indicative of what the industrialized city is doing to old England is the "frightful" memory of a patch of grassless and littered ground against the background of smoke-darkened houses and an "interminable vista of factory chimneys."[85] Even in a work patriotically celebrating English life, "The English People," written in 1944, Orwell cannot refrain from noting that "whole counties" are being turned into "blackened deserts" because of industrialization, and the kind of Oz resulting from the urbanization accompanying the proliferation of plants and factories, from the "seas of yellow brick" spreading out across the countryside, is one with fewer and fewer "ancient monuments."[86] When George Bowling of *Coming Up for Air* does return to the scene of his Edwardian youth, when Lower Binfield was a small town surrounded by open country, he is stunned at the disappearance of his remembered past beneath an "enormous river of brand-new houses." A once secluded pastoral setting now lies buried beneath the "volcanic eruption" of the expanding city suburbs (211, 235).

In *Burmese Days* the clash between the old and the new can be viewed as the colonial encounter between the harmoniously pastoral world of traditional Asia and the servants of a modern, urbanized utopia. Willingly and consciously or not, the whites, including even Flory, are the agents of an imperial process making available the resources of the East for the urban civilization of the West. And although motivated to come to the East by a desire to find health and peace of mind through a life lived closer to nature, they themselves are engaged in a collective assault on their colonial environment. "Trees and men do not grow together," says Kipling's python Kaa to Mowgli as they view the tree roots that have pushed their way down through the stone floor of a city only after its abandonment to the jungle by its human inhabitants (*Jungle Book*, 160). By the time of the events described in *Burmese Days*, 1923 or 1924, Kaa's statement still makes sense, although its specific application is reversed: now man is triumphant over the forests. The Flory who in his jungle-enclosed pool feels himself returning to the condition of natural man is also the agent of a timber firm engaged in a process which, Flory predicts, will end in a Burma "shaved flat" (142). An image Orwell used several years later to illustrate the dystopian cultural dismemberment resulting from two centuries of intellectual rebellion against accepted beliefs—the Western intellectuals' plunge into the political horrors of the present after having "sawed and sawed and sawed at the branch" on which they have been sitting[87]—suggests the alienating effects of the European colonial system. The sawing in which Flory and the other white colonials are engaged is producing artifacts that are becoming substitutes for the natural. The image that dominates Flory's most frenzied diatribe against the imperialist ideal of material progress is the gramophone. His contempt for European civilization reaches a Flaubertian intensity in his denunciation of the Western "swinery of gramophones," and at the center of his guilt-laden vision of the future is a Burma covered with villas equipped with gramophones, their cases the product of the land's deforestation, "all . . . playing the same tune" (42). The first sign of this transformation is the concrete tennis court where the members of the European Club encircle a gramophone playing, appropriately, "Show Me the Way to Go Home"; and the extent to which Flory's ties with the premodern East are weakened by his own participation in imperialist exploitation is shown by his willingness to sweeten the pot of married life in Burma by promising Elizabeth Lackersteen a gramophone of her own (180, 210). For Mowgli, in Kipling's *Jungle Book*, the time comes when henceforth the "jungle is shut." In *Burmese Days* the despairing wail of Ma Hla May, "how can I go back?" (153), is a collective cry of grief—that not only of the colonialized Asian but also of Orwell's more sensitive English characters—at the alienating effects of modernization.

Although not blind to the benefits of mechanization, Orwell usually attacks the machine, or more precisely the frame of mind that denigrates nature while enthusiastically envisioning a future of increasing technological sophistication and power. Of the various sources for the early twentieth-century confidence in the socially melioristic effects of a scientifically managed society, two thinkers loom especially large in Orwell's writings. With the basic writings of one of them, H. G. Wells, Orwell was quite familiar; his knowledge of the other, Marx, was, says Bernard Crick, "secondary."[88] Although surely aware of the Fabian Wells's criticism of the violence practiced by contemporary Marxist-Leninists and their dismissive attitude toward him, Orwell is more concerned with ideas shared by Wellsian utopianism and communism regarding the control of the natural environment. As stated by Christopher Caudwell, a British Marxist theoretician writing in the thirties, under communism human freedom is to be attained through the organization of society for a decisive "struggle with Nature," a collective effort to gain "mastery" over it—and with mastery, liberation.[89] Although Caudwell's works may not have come to Orwell's attention, Orwell did know John Strachey and, among other writings by him, almost surely read this leftist's seminal work on communism, *The Coming Struggle for Power,* which envisions a classless society finally able to turn its "entire energies to the subjugation of [its] oldest antagonist, nature."[90] In the futurist outlook of the English scientist and communist J. D. Bernal, writing in 1929, phenomenal nature is something to be transcended and left behind in man's scientific and technical progress. Advances in molecular physics and chemistry will produce materials unknown in nature, and in time populations will live in giant sealed globes, self-contained environments unaffected by the weather outside or the earth's gravitational pull.[91]

Referred to by Orwell as the "father of 'Scientification,'"[92] H. G. Wells is, in Orwell's eyes, the one person most responsible for the increasing reliance on mechanization by twentieth-century socialists. The "now familiar Wellsian Utopia," Orwell notes disapprovingly in *The Road to Wigan Pier,* is the end product of mechanization, with "machines to save work, machines to save thought, machines to save pain" (193). In one of Wells's most famous early utopian works, *A Modern Utopia* (1904), applied science is presented as mankind's royal road to freedom from his ages-long enslavement to the soil. Turning a cold eye on the agricultural labor-intensive utopias of the distant past and more recent "Return-to-Nature" utopias, Wells places his narrator in an excitingly innovative society, the scientific advances of which will put a halt to the "digging [of] potatoes . . . day after day"[93]—a synecdoche for mankind's history of physical toil.

Trotsky claimed for electricity a key role in the Bolsheviks' ascent to power, and Bertrand Russell once called to the attention of his readers Lenin's conviction that continued Bolshevik control would depend in large part on the electrification of agriculture.[94] In *Animal Farm* the windmill comes to embody the hope for a scientifically run community. After having read Jones's technical magazines, Snowball is bedazzled by the vision of a streamlined futuristic farm society in which "electricity" would not only run all the farm machinery but also provide the barn and hen house with warmth, lighting, and "hot . . . water" (45).

Carried a step farther, several critics' view of Snowball's windmill as symbolizing the quixotic folly of attempting to construct a fully mechanized society[95] leads to an observation relevant to the place of the horse in Western civilization—that technological modernization, like the tilting at a windmill, is likely to separate man from horse. Certainly the horse is on Orwell's short list of favored creatures, and his juxtaposition of equine and human being suggests that the latter might gain from the animal's proximity a share of its characteristic virtues, such as Boxer's mixture of gentleness and endurance. Thus in *Down and Out in Paris and London* Orwell's retrospective description of a pastoral scene, a meadow where tramps are accustomed to gather, juxtaposes two implicitly related elements—the animal in the form of "two carthorse colts" grazing in the field, and the human, a tramp with two names, his own first name and the heroic appellation "Hercules" that the narrator bestows on him (198).

But the prestige of the horse had slipped in Orwell's lifetime, and by the time of the 1930s it is no longer considered a fair trade for a kingdom. In *The Road to Wigan Pier* Orwell mentions a confidential remark made to him by a man "prominent" in the Independent Labor party regarding the latter's liking for horses. The sense of shame that Orwell claims to have detected in the man's statement serves as the basis for a generalization about the difference between past and present: "Horses, you see, belong to the vanished agricultural past, and all sentiment for the past carries with it a vague smell of heresy" (201–2). The attitude toward the horse as a reflection of changing attitudes toward the past is exemplified in the reaction to the animal of two late nineteenth-century writers—Gerard Manley Hopkins, whom Orwell regards as essentially a man of the past, and H. G. Wells, herald of the modern age. The imaginative creation of a man from "rural communities . . . still distinctly similar to what they had been in Saxon times," the cart horse in Hopkins's poem "Felix Randall" is a "magnificent mythical beast," the presence of which raises an obscure village suicide "to the plane of tragedy."[96] On the other hand, what Orwell regards as Wells's inadequacy as a social and political thinker, his insensitivity to the military enthusiasms that have molded history much more than scientific rationality, is indicated by the markedly hostile attitude toward the horse expressed in his early works.[97]

The tension in *Animal Farm* between the farm community's rooted attachment to the agricultural past and the imperative toward modernization is most vividly expressed through the bipolar imagery of windmill, particularly the electrification process that depends on it, and horse. It may be frivolous to suggest a covert pun linking Snowball, the porker whose idea it is to erect the windmill as the center of a future technological utopia, with the theoretical founder of modern applied science, Francis Bacon, who in *New Atlantis* envisions, among other technological marvels, "engines for multiplying and enforcing of winds, to set also agoing divers motions."[98] In any event, as icon of the new age of mechanical power, the windmill stands as a threat to the existence of the old age of literal horse power.

Criticizing the backwardness of existing economic policies, Wells refers to man as still prone to behavior exhibiting the "infinite wastefulness of his mother Nature."[99] The aging mare Clover is one in a line of maternally natural figures appearing here and there in Orwell's works, the reminders of a vital and caring past at odds with the values and goals of the present. She is the Burmese prostitute, a "fat, good-tempered creature," on whose shoulder Flory boyishly weeps after being rejected by Elizabeth in *Burmese Days* (223); the "Toby jug of a woman, with monstrous breasts," who, toward the end of the hop-picking episode in *A Clergyman's Daughter,* loudly but futilely tries to stop the law from arresting her son as accessory to one of Nobby's thefts (139); in *Keep the Aspidistra Flying,* "Mother Meakin," a "jelly-soft old creature," whose lodging house is Gordon Comstock's temporary refuge from the inexorable claims of the money world (207); the memory of George Bowling's mother merged with the fading recollection of agricultural England throughout the central portion of *Coming Up for Air*; and in *Nineteen Eighty-Four* the wide-hipped old prole woman brutally silenced by the police and the imprisoned "enormous wreck of a woman . . . with great tumbling breasts" (221, 231)—the hero's real or archetypal mother.

In *Animal Farm* two types of pastoral existences stand opposed in the forms of, on the one hand, the electricity-produced warmth of the technological utopia, and, on the other, the physical warmth of Clover. At the same time in which Old Major, marginalizing the significance of the long-forgotten memory of his mother by focusing attention to the present and the future, is attempting to turn the farm animals into political activists, the "stout motherly" Clover provides a warm and restorative presence enabling some of the animals—the duckling dozing between the "wall" of her sturdy legs and the purring cat nestled beside her—to remain oblivious to Old Major's polemic (4). Downcast at the sight of the destroyed windmill, once the source of their self-admiration, and reduced to bewilderment by the slaughter of fellow animals during the bloody show trial to affix blame for the disaster, the humbler animals instinctively turn to Clover. "Huddled" around her, the animals are able to ward off utter despair by fleeting memories of the farm as a happier place (73). However, like other maternal figures, Clover's powers are limited, declining. Clover's motherly concern at the younger Mollie's willingness to accept sweets from human strangers results only in the latter's irritation and flight from the farm (42–43). That political expediency outweighs the claims of biological motherhood is indicated by Napoleon's taking away from the bitches Jessie and Bluebell their newborn pups to make them totally dependent on and thereby loyal to him (29). And in line with the suggestion made earlier in this chapter, for the purposely inebriated and thus sexually impotent Farmer Jones the female snoring in his bed is no longer the sexually expectant if not aggressive wife but a passively maternal presence. Perhaps contributing to Jones's demoralization and decline after his expulsion from the farm is the severance of his connection with the maternal, his exile from the mother soil and apparent loss of the mother-wife, and it is this primitive deprivation that may motivate the accelerated drinking that eventually wins him the embrace of an institutional (and presumably authoritarian) mother-surrogate—the "inebriates' home" where he ends his days (106). As for Clover's decline, having nursed Boxer back to a fragile state of health after his collapse from overwork on the reconstruction of the windmill, the mare is unable to prevent his shipment to the horse slaughterer's, and toward the end of the narrative the information that her "old eyes" are growing dimmer (73, 112) serves as a reminder of the aging beast's mortality.

If Clover's diminishing power in the farm community signifies an England (as well as a Russia) in danger of losing touch with a maternally nourishing past, Boxer's sacrificial breakdown in the service of what he and the other worker animals believe to be technological progress might be interpreted as allegorically portending the future deterioration of the animal community. Years earlier, in *Road to Wigan Pier*, Orwell made much of the harmful effects of industrialism on the population as a whole. Geared for the mass production of "cheap substitutes for everything," modern industry is responsible for the "physical degeneracy of modern England" (97, 98). Orwell's language suggests that the deterioration is of the character as well as the flesh, for industrialism makes life too "safe and soft." And here as elsewhere the decline is imaged in the separation of the man from the mount: "the result of the transition from horses to cars has been an increase in human softness" (195). The final condition of Boxer, inside the van about to carry him to the knacker's in exchange for money needed to continue work on the windmill, emblematically conveys a message close to the spirit of Orwell's earlier warning: "The time had been when a few kicks from Boxer's hoofs would have smashed the van to matchwood. But alas! his strength had left him; and in a few moments the sound of drumming hoofs grew fainter and died away" (102).

6

"THAT INFERNAL PALAEOLITHIC SKULL"
The Myth of the New Man

For the progressive thinker of the 1930s, the West was moving into a new, happier age, and coming into view on the horizon of this dawning age of progress was the New Man (presumably followed a step behind by the New Woman) recognizable—depending on the specific progressive social philosophy touching fingers with him like Michelangelo's deity and Adam on the ceiling of the Sistine chapel—by the crisp and functional uniform of the forward-looking airman, the hero of some Wellsian utopias; the white laboratory smock of the scientist busy creating synthetic foods and materials and fuels; or the Marxist-Leninist worker-revolutionary's plain cloth cap.

Eschewing the nineteenth-century glorification of the individual as the fashioner of his own social destiny, the New Man embraces a collective identity. As described in F. J. Sheed's *Communism and Man* (favorably reviewed by Orwell in January 1939), the citizen of the perfected Marxist society "will conceive of himself only as a member of society and will be quite incapable of pursuing (because quite incapable of conceiving) individual ends as distinct from the collective purpose. . . . Man will have been completely socialised and will be incapable of any action other than social action."[100] In H. G. Wells's futuristically speculative *The Shape of Things to Come,* events taking place between the nineteenth century and the twenty-first produce a new man who is "far more social and unselfish in his ideology and mental habits" than his forebears—a man so changed as to be a "different animal."[101]

The New Man of the progressivist thinkers will be rational and in control of his primitive, socially disruptive instincts. In the world state described in *The Shape of Things to Come,* ritual displays of superstitiousness have vanished, and the new people are no longer in the grip of such compulsions as gluttony, lust, or a passion for gambling; rather they have been turned into rationally self-controlled hedonists.[102] In *The Coming Struggle for Power* Strachey sees the collectivization of desire under communism—the willingness of the citizenry to work in order to support and improve the new economic system—as revealing an "immense fund of constructive idealism"[103]. If in *The Road to Wigan Pier* Orwell's irritated portrayal of the Wellsian "little fat men" (210) appears somewhat overstated, Orwell's reference to the human "brain in the bottle" as the "logical end of mechanical progress" (201) seems positively Swiftian in its grotesqueness. However, in 1929 the scientist J. D. Bernal put forward an idea almost identical with Orwell's bottled brain: the almost limitless expansion of an individual's thought processes could be effected by a separation of brain from body and the indefinite attachment of the former to an artificial life-support system contained within a cylinder[104].

"A pig may be educated"—so the narrator, Prendick, of Wells's *The Island of Doctor Moreau,* states as one of the doctor's basic assumptions. Moreau's laboratory experimentation on the animals he has shipped to his island, combined with the prohibitory "Law" the more or less humanized beasts must memorize and obey to the letter, is designed to produce a mental as well as physical metamorphosis— to make the unwilling subjects of his bloody, painful experiments not only look like human beings but also think like them.

- 68 -

"That Infernal Palaeolithic Skull"

Although Moreau's acts of vivisectionist violence eventually back-fire, leaving him dead and his creatures on the way back to a condition of savagery, the impression conveyed by the twentieth-century pro-gressivist intellectual is that now his understanding of history is so comprehensive that even the violent deed can be shown to have a place in a larger developmental pattern. As a Fabian theorist, Moreau's cre-ator could claim that the modern socialist shares the scientist's "faith in the order, the knowableness of things and the power of men . . . to overcome chance," although with the socialist this sense of power in-cludes an ability to conceive of a "comprehensive design for all the social activities of man."[105] Wells's own Noah, the hero of *All Aboard for Ararat* (1940), is confident he can refashion post-Deluge humanity, the survivors of World War II, by applying the principles of scientific behaviorism. In the works of twentieth-century English communist or communist-leaning theorists—Christopher Caudwell, John Strachey, Harold J. Laski, G. D. H. Cole, and others—there is no doubt that now, because of Marx, the underlying laws governing the historical development of capitalist society and its present functioning are discernible.

The implication of all this is that history is an evolutionary pro-cess that has finally produced thinkers and leaders who, because of their expanded historical awareness, can guide the masses in effecting those more or less radical social and political changes of existing sys-tems in order to establish a new, rationally structured and functioning society.

That this new society has little or no use for the natural man, the late-born romantic, is indicated by the unflattering portrayal of that type in Wells's *A Modern Utopia*—the "Voice of Nature," a garrulous and giggling "creature of pose and vanity" mindlessly denouncing roads, houses, and any other evidence of utopian planning that sepa-rates man from the green world[106]. Although in *Coming Up for Air* Orwell appropriates this old man to satirize the inauthenticity of the 1930s antimodernist whose idea of being close to nature involves veg-etarianism, nudist parties, and fake Tudor housing developments (253–54), elsewhere in Orwell there are more serious and troubling signs of twentieth-century man's problematic relationship with nature. "We love animals," notes the art historian Kenneth Clark, "we watch them with delight, we study their habits with ever-increasing curiosity; and we destroy them. We have sacrificed them to the gods, we have killed them in arenas to enjoy a cruel excitement, we still hunt them and we slaughter them by the million out of greed."[107] In Orwell the alienation of man from nature is most tellingly expressed by man's violent treatment of it. Anticipating Boxer's fate in *Animal Farm* and the explanation about the origin of the fable in the remembered scene of an English farm boy whipping a cart horse forward,[108] is the reference in *Down and Out in Paris and London* to the wretched existence of the typical Far Eastern gharry pony, galled by sores, cruelly lashed by its driver, and finally sold for slaughter (117–28). In the essay "Marrakech" (December 1939) the angry description of the way that Moroccans slowly kill their faithful donkeys by cruel overloading leads to the confession that this rather than human suffering is what "makes one's blood boil"[109].

Stories of animal vengeance reflect, it is claimed, man's uneasiness not only at his specific acts of cruelty to animals but also at the fact of animals' general condition of victimization.[110] Despite the many references to animals in Orwell's narratives, the only one in which there is a sustained relationship between man and beast—that of Flory and his dog, Flo, in *Burmese Days*—ends violently, with Flory shooting his pet to death before taking his own life (281). Presumably a reader is expected to infer the likelihood of another kind of life-negating conclusion to the figuratively human-animal relationship in *A Clergyman's Daughter*, that between the surname Hare and its clerical bearer—the sonless and misogynistic widower who will probably do nothing to keep the family name alive.

MAN AGAINST ANIMAL

As a general rule in Orwell's works, the relationship between man and animal becomes less tense and problematic as the distance increases between them. Orwell's delighted spotting of the signs of living nature high atop some buildings in a Spanish town, the swallows' nests he notices only after the termination of his front-line service during the Spanish Civil War, are valuable reminders to the ex-combatant of his now returning sense of humanity (*Homage to Catalonia*, 203). But a bird in the hand, such as the beautiful jungle pigeon shot and later held by Flory and Elizabeth Lackersteen in *Burmese Days*, is simply dead (165, 167). The wild creatures in Gustave Flaubert's "The Legend of St. Julien the Hospitaller"—the mouse lured by hunger to within striking distance of young Julien, the unsuspecting pigeon felled and then strangled by the ecstatic youth (a scene that could be the model for Elizabeth's rapturous embrace of the pigeon she has shot), and the scores of other animal victims of his perversity—learn a hard lesson about the danger of sharing physical space with man. That the laying hens in *Animal Farm* are learning this lesson in regard to their humanoid leaders is shown by their brave but doomed protest against Napoleon's expropriation of newly laid eggs—their flight to the henhouse rafters. Later the folly of not heeding the precept of prudential distancing is demonstrated when the leaders of the brief revolt make the double mistake of confessing to the near approach of Snowball (through their dreams) while standing within pouncing distance of Napoleon's bloodthirsty dogs (65, 71).

As the initial success of Jones's invasion of the animal-controlled farm turns into a rout, the ousted farmer's own Bay of Pigs, the beasts counterattack as a unified, single-minded group, so united in their resolve to rid their space of humanity that "even the cat suddenly leapt off a roof onto a cowman's shoulders and sank her claws in his neck" (36). Perhaps the cat's attack on the hybrid, the cowman, is a rage reaction triggered by the scent of terror she has picked up from earlier animals that have been violated in one way or another by contact with man—the smell that would have been given off by the tormented, anguished puma-woman created and eventually destroyed by Wells's Dr. Moreau or by the "writhing" and "sobbing" leopard shot by Flory and Elizabeth and later reincarnated in the pathetic figure of the "kittenish" Ma Hla May squirming on the floor before her faithless lover in *Burmese Days* (154–55, 172) with a self-abasement totally foreign to the feline nature.

Dozing during the speech by Old Major that is meant to politically radicalize the animals, the purring cat seems to be displaying an indifference to the boar's revolutionary exhortation as dense as the wall of snoring separating Mrs. Jones from her husband in the nearby bedroom, and later, making herself scarce just before Napoleon's exhibition of terrorism against fellow animals—a quantum leap from revolutionary idealism to tyranny—the cat seems to know in her bones that political power-hunger and innocent animality do not mix. She is, however, not the first animal to have sensed this. In *All Aboard for Ararat* a water vole sits by a stream listening to the sounds of Wells's Noah soliloquizing about the post-Deluge world state he plans to establish, and just at the point when he refers to the antitraditional intellectual elite that are to take control, the rodent, an "unconvinced individualist," leaps into the stream to escape the approaching danger (81–82).

In *Burmese Days* it is the figure emerging from a river and leaping into the compound of the military police, the Flory whom events have transformed from nature-loving isolate to semipolitical hero on a mission to save the whites besieged in their club by rioting natives, that sends some stalled horses into a panic (251). Perhaps as a check on any tendency to idealize the violence of the Spanish Civil War, Orwell implies in *Homage to Catalonia* that the revolutionary spirit has not made the lives of equines any better than earlier, before the time when a certain cavalry barracks was renamed after Lenin and its horses sent to the front (7). The care taken by an Aragonese farmer for his mules is balanced by what Orwell clearly regards as the shockingly cruel treatment of donkeys, kicked in the testicles to move them forward (41). Although the civil war has put a stop to bullfighting, "splendid" Spanish cavalry horses are being ridden "to death" by young militiamen (18). Like a fragment from Picasso's *Guernica* is a passage in one of Orwell's literary notebooks entered sometime between 1939 and 1947. In the course of a World War I battle a youth too hesitantly whipping a horse (apparently hitched up to a piece of field artillery) to make it stand up and move is replaced by an older, sturdier, and more ruthlessly efficient soldier: "The whip screams as it flies through the air. . . . At last with a scream the dying horse struggles to its feet & the gun . . . moves slowly."[111] Although Orwell's own dog may have been none the worse for being named Marx, a dog branded with the initials of one of the Spanish Civil War political factions is described as having "slunk along as though conscious that there was something wrong" (*Homage to Catalonia*, 18). And reacting neurotically as dogs do when under excessive stress, some canines in a London air raid "go wild and savage . . . and have . . . to be shot."[112]

The various types of assaults on nature described in Orwell's works, from the blighting of a natural landscape to specific acts of violence against animals, are the signs of an unhealthy inner condition that is threatening to get out of control. "In the dark evening, after a quite idle day," observes the Orwellian narrator in *Burmese Days* in describing the quality of the white colonial's life in the East, "one's ennui reaches a pitch that is frantic, suicidal. Work, prayer, books, drinking, talking—they are all powerless against it; it can only be sweated out through the pores of the skin" (56). For some, those driven close to the edge of nihilistic despair and self-destruction by persistent reminders of personal futility and emptiness, the only activity that can be relied on to produce a cathartic sweating is that pursued by Flaubert's blood-obsessed Julien—the stalking of animals. It seems to be the unspoken assumption of both Flory and Elizabeth that not just the sweaty effort of the hunt but also the killing it leads to will transform the troubled, overly civilized Westerner into the amorally vital and powerful hunter—in much the same way that the consumption of a slain leopard's inner organs is supposed to endow the natives with the animal's strength (174). With the body of their own slain leopard being carried ahead of them and "both their shirts . . . drenched with sweat," Flory and Elizabeth are able to break through the isolating walls of their usual self-defensiveness and share an intense moment of emotional unity as the great white stalkers—Nimrods under the skin. The dog Flo, as though sensing in the dead leopard a fate in store for itself, keeps her distance from the procession, "slinking . . . a long way in the rear" (166, 173–74).

Accompanying the impulse to hunt down and kill is another impulse, the desire to touch an animal, to close the distance between man and a thing of nature. Holding a freshly shot pigeon, Elizabeth of *Burmese Days* experiences an emotion far more intense than any feeling she might have toward a human being: "she could hardly give it up, the feel of it so ravished her" (167). In *Animal Farm* there are here and there signs that within Jones the proprietor—the economic man routinely castrating young animals and putting to death old and therefore unprofitable beasts (8, 18)—exists a natural man longing to return to a pastoral condition. An ousted and humiliated Jones may sit in the Red Lion and complain about the injustice done to him, but unlike other farmers in the area, he refrains from spreading malicious stories about the rebels, such as the tales of cannibalism, fiendish tortures, and sexual promiscuity (32–33). More revealing is the fact that the violence to which his animals were once subjected—the castrations, the throat-slittings, the tying of weights around the necks of beasts to be drowned—involved the physical closeness of man and animal. And although there are hired hands on the prerevolutionary Manor Farm, Old Major's speech indicates that Jones has performed these tasks himself (8). Jones contains within himself the pastoral impulse toward submergence in nature and the antipastoral need to own and master nature.

In the India of Kipling's imagination, violence often serves the cause of a justice broad enough to accommodate human codes and jungle law. In *The Jungle Book* the destructive power of the wild animal and the human demand for retributive justice work together as the elephant Hathi and his sons, at Mowgli's behest, pound back into the ground a village in which the boy's mother was shamefully abused. But in an age when violence is increasingly in the service of political power, it is not easy to tell believable stories of animal energy and human purpose jointly striving toward an end accommodating the needs of both.

"That Infernal Palaeolithic Skull"

In Orwell's much-anthologized elephant essay, "Shooting an Elephant" (1936), the emphasis is on the tragically discordant relationship between animal nature and the paradoxes of imperial rule. What turns the policeman's routine investigation into a grisly blood sport is an inner alienation from nature that becomes increasingly overt. In the same instance that one aspect of the earlier self being recalled by the narrator, the humane Orwell who feels a kinship with nature, is determined not to shoot the creature, another Orwell, the colonial policeman who must always appear powerful and in control, is mentally reducing it to something inorganic—a "huge and costly piece of machinery" and a "steam-roller."[113] The first rifle Orwell carries, old and not powerful enough to bring down an elephant, betokens his intention of only observing. But a few moments later his holding of another rifle—a "beautiful German thing with cross-hair sights" that the natives view as "magical"—transforms him from "conjuror" to a being conjured up—the elephant's stalker.[114] The final stage of the transformation of the living into the mechanical occurs when the great beast's dying gasps become the "ticking of a clock."[115]

The dying elephant's sounds are measuring the interval between one empire, the relatively benign but expiring British Empire, and a more ruthlessly efficient successor. Also being marked is the disappearance of the older imperialist, at least grudgingly willing to kill a valuable animal to prevent further loss of native life, and the entry onto the stage of modern political history of the new man, heralded here by the "younger men" certain that a coolie is less valuable than an elephant. However, it may well be that Orwell the writer is mindful of a lesson to be learned from the readings of young Eric Blair—that the new man, rational and coldly efficient, may in fact be a very old breed in disguise. As Kipling's Mowgli learns in the first *Jungle Book*, the object once used to guide nature's energy along the path of "Man's Law," the bejeweled elephant goad that the boy takes from the treasure trove guarded by the White Cobra, has now reverted to an instrument of barbaric impulse, its theft having resulted in the violent deaths of six men in one night. A shocked Mowgli vows "never again" to "bring into the Jungle strange things." The strange thing brought into the jungle of the East is the armed might of Western imperialism. The "backbone" of imperial rule is the army, Flory claims in *Burmese Days*, and to this force is added the intimidating power of the "durable jails" dotting the empire and the white man's willingness to flog the native—as even Flory, critic of empire, threatens to do to Ma Hla May to silence her questions about Elizabeth Lackersteen—and to gun them down with sufficient provocation (18, 68–69, 87, 112). It is a mark of either callousness or naiveté that Flory, quick to congratulate Elizabeth on a shot that cripples a leopard, expresses surprise at the Burmans' violent reaction to a system resting on physical force (173, 249).

Like the German-made weapon in "Shooting an Elephant," there is something magical about the gun in *Animal Farm,* an instrument exerting a strangely maleficent influence over the course of the revolution. Those who take up the gun, whether human being or animal, are ruled—and in time ruined—by it. Although the explosion of Farmer Jones's gun out of the bedroom window seems to be the loud assertion of his supreme power, the pellets hitting the barn are in effect marking the spot, or at least the structure, where will soon appear the "Seven Commandments" proclaiming the liberation of Manor Farm from human control (12, 21). Adding to the weapon's aura of mysterious potency, its mana, is its subtle but firm hold on the minds and feelings of the very beings, the farm animals, who should most fear its spell. Moreover, it appears that the gun escapes from the tale-teller's control: the description of the events preceding Jones's initial ouster—his awakening from a boozy slumber in the parlor downstairs (not in the bedroom where the gun is kept); his rushing to the shed, armed, we are told, with a whip, not a gun; his and his employees' hurried exit from the farm; and the wife's equally rushed escape with only what she can carry in a "carpet bag" (16–17)—implies that the shotgun is still in the house when the human residents flee. If so, then it may be that so frightening is the gun that its presence is to be excluded from the consciousness of the liberated animals. Of all the objects of human dominance in house or outbuilding for the freed animals to view with distaste and righteously reject—from castrating knives and dog-chains to ribbons (17–18)—the one strangely not mentioned is the gun. A book by Bertrand Russell reviewed by Orwell in January 1939, *Power: A New Social Analysis* (1938), refers to the modern tendency to base power on mechanisms, including mechanized weaponry. Perhaps it is to avoid the temptation of this kind of power that Orwell veils the ominous piece from the animals' sight. However, the repressed will return, and eventually this weapon—or a weapon— forces its way into the beasts' awareness when Jones counterattacks armed with a shotgun that he leaves behind on a dunghill when the invasion is beaten back (38).

At this point in *Animal Farm* begin two important developments. First, like a slain and resurrected deity, the gun that earlier disappeared through a crack in the narrative reappears, as though emerging from the muck, to become an important feature of the triumphant beasts' celebratory ritual: "It was decided to set the gun up at the foot of the flagstaff, like a piece of artillery, and to fire it twice a year—once on October the twelfth, the anniversary of the Battle of the Cowshed, and once on Midsummer Day, the anniversary of the Rebellion" (38). Second, it is at this point that the simplicity of the animals' early postrevolutionary existence takes on a labyrinthine complexity, with the divisiveness and distrust arising from Snowball's scheme for a second, technological revolution. Before the weapon's appearance, luck, ancient Fortuna, seems to be on the side of the animals: having destroyed the reminders of Jones's rule, they sing "Beasts of England" "seven times running," and the same lucky number appears again soon afterward in the Seven Commandments, in which are codified the ethical absolutes of the new order (18, 21). However, before long the seven rules are casuistically subverted, and finally the gun, at first ritually fired only twice, takes control of Fortune, its seven firings celebrating a lie—that the destruction wrought by Frederick's bloody invasion was somehow a great victory for the animals (89).

During the battle with the Nazi-like Frederick, something takes place—the goring of an invading man's stomach "by a cow's horn"

(87)—that hints at the existence of a Minotaur's cave at the center of the revolutionary labyrinth. In *The Island of Doctor Moreau* the scientist is never able to check the persistent drift of his experimental creatures back toward their original animality; and more radically subversive is Prendick's uneasy intimation of a connection between the veiled bestiality of the creatures on the island and something similar in his own (perhaps ancestral) past. This uneasiness mounts to terror at the shadowy thing whose movement through the dark forest is an "echo" of the civilized Englishman's footsteps across star-illuminated open ground. In *Burmese Days* the external, purely animal threat to Elizabeth, the "huge buffalo" with "crescent-shaped horns" (79), becomes in *A Clergyman's Daughter* the "buffalo-like man" with a crescent-shaped moustache who participates in Mrs. Creevy's humiliation of Dorothy Hare for explaining to her students the reference in *MacBeth* to Macduff's having been "untimely ripp'd" from the womb (249–50, 252). Curiously, Orwell's beast fable contains the most extensive dramatization of violence of all his narratives, more even than *Homage to Catalonia* and *Nineteen Eighty-Four,* and it is in the fable that the horned bovine, the allegorical representation of politicized man, becomes overtly violent—first smashing in Jones's shed door to set the revolution in motion (16) and finally goring a human foe.

Doubts About Natural Man

"Old Mattu," the "earth-coloured" Burman who, lacking any sense of calendar time, thinks he is a youngster; the innocent, nature-loving side of Flory that makes him seem a "boy still" (*Burmese Days,* 43–44, 50); the physically "splendid" miners working in the very depths of the earth, much of the time "on all fours . . . like dogs" (*The Road to Wigan Pier,* 23, 29); the various maternal figures in Orwell's narratives—these characters, among others, belong to the category of contemporary natural man, a type defined by its position on a border between twentieth-century civilization and a pastoral condition of animal simplicity and vitality. However, in the political reality of the 1930s, the frontier was the place where dangerous military "incidents" were taking place, and in the literature of the period the border motif comes to be associated with imminent violence and violation. Even in Orwell's treatment of a character that appears to be the quintessential natural man, Nobby, Dorothy Hare's companion on the way to the Kentish hop fields in *A Clergyman's Daughter,* there are disturbing signs that the animal within the human being is more menacing than amiable. Able to sleep contentedly in a patch of wet grass as a bed, quick to root around under hedges for firewood to boil tea, which, we are told, he can brew even in the most severe weather (109, 117)—he appears to strike a fine balance between the natural and the civilized, between modern, urbanized man and traditional agricultural Englishman. However, alerted by the name of a dog owned by a Knype Hill woman, "Toto" (17), we may suspect that in Nobby—with his resemblance to an "ape," "orang-outang," and his "simian face" (100–1, 109)—flows the blood of the "Winged Monkeys," servants of an evil witch in *The Wizard of Oz,* who savage the companions of Frank Baum's Dorothy. When Nobby is arrested, part of the loot found in his hut consists of apples, a sign that a pastoral Eden is about to be lost. But the crime that is really responsible for his expulsion from the imperfect but humanly appealing golden age paradise of the hop-picking community (and not only Nobby's expulsion but also that of the youth he has involved in the theft) is the depredation that in *Animal Farm* Farmer Jones thinks he is preventing when he fires the gun out the bedroom window—a raid on the henhouse. More specifically, Nobby has shed blood: as the arresting policeman says, "exhibit B, some blood-stained chicken feathers" (139). Thus, from relatively innocent and harmless gatherer Nobby has turned into a hunter, a killer and shedder of blood.

Referring to the hunting episode in *Burmese Days,* a critic concludes that Orwell's characters inhabit a "post-Darwinian world" where a "basis for fascist ethics can be found in nature" as well as in society.[116] In the early 1940s Edwin Muir, noted translator of Franz

Kafka's works, judged fascism and Nazism as more fully committed to the idea of the "natural man" than even communism.[117] Aside from the military threat to Great Britain posed by the Axis powers, the doctrines of fascism and Nazism, as well as the actual brutalities committed in accordance with the letter and the spirit of these beliefs, can be seen as a rebuttal to the progressive view of history. The rise of fascism in its various forms from Italy to Japan in the second and third decades of the twentieth century, and in particular the appearance of National Socialism in Germany, introduced a new factor into the Orwellian bipolar reality of pastoral naturalness and urban industrial utopianism. In its celebration of swift, brutal action, the Western European authoritarian parties and ideologies offered in place of the myth of pastoral calm and goodness a vision of nature as ruthless and warlike. The roar of the whole German industrial system turning out tanks and bombers for the next war was loud enough to awaken some liberal-progressive sleepers from their dreams of a rational, just, and democratic future.

Complicating Orwell's imaginative endeavor to conjure up a believable image of natural man, at once vital and benign, from beneath the asphalt of modern industrialized and urbanized England are disturbing intimations of a much older and more primitive secret sharer of the human psyche—a proto-totalitarian homunculus that could outgrow and engulf its containing environment. The naturalistic basis for Hitler's vision of reality is repeatedly indicated in *Mein Kampf*, reviewed by Orwell in March 1940. In support of one of his key ideas, racial purity, Hitler appeals to what he claims is a basic principle of Nature—the "inner seclusion" of each species in "Nature's garden."[118] Bestowing a biological inevitability on the racist violence to come, Hitler emphasizes "certain corrective decisions" that "Nature has the habit of making" to insure racial purity, and it is implied that *Mein Kampf* contains the kind of "perceptive knowledge" that can compensate for the Germans' lost natural, instinctive ability to reject racial hybridization.[119] Somehow a prophylactic against racial "bastardization" is Hitler's concept of "Germanization," defined in terms of a national closeness to land first conquered by Germans and then settled by German peasantry.[120] Hitler's almost mystical attitude toward the land probably contributed to the formulation of the National Socialist back-to-the soil policy to increase the German farm population—details of which appear in Robert Brady's *The Spirit and Structure of German Fascism* (1937), a book in Orwell's personal library. The reference in Borkenau's *The Totalitarian Enemy* to the Nazi longing for an innocently pagan oneness with nature resembles the need felt by Orwell's characters to escape the burden of modern consciousness by a return to a more primitive pastoral condition.

One reason why the period between the wars, and especially the thirties, is labeled an age of anxiety is the blurring of ideological and ethical identities, the tendency for progressive aspirations to take on the darker hues of the reactionary opposition—the fascist black and the Nazi brown. Even before the appearance of these atavistic movements, alarms were sounded regarding Bolshevism. In 1920 Bertrand Russell, not unsympathetic with Soviet ideals, warned that revolutionary violence sets free a "wild beast" in the victors,[121] and Harold J. Laski, more leftist than Russell, described communist revolutionary activism as a form of "savagery" that, once let loose, would be "utterly destructive of . . . a decent existence."[122] In the words of John McGovern, a representative of the British Independent Labor party in Spain to report on the persecution of working-class leaders by communists: "These [communist] German and Italian officials who escaped from Hitler and Mussolini have now themselves adopted the Fascist methods of brutality."[123] Agreeing with Borkenau's characterization in *The Totalitarian Enemy* of Trotsky as the "arch-Fascist" whose pupil, Stalin, has been a model for totalitarian Germany, Orwell notes in his review the tendency of any totalitarian regime, right or left, to lash out in any direction, against foe and supposed friend alike, to secure power.

In the essay "Wells, Hitler and the World State" Orwell faults the author of *The Outline of History* for his glib optimism about the future, for failing to see that now "ideas appropriate to the Stone Age" are being implemented by German technology.[124] In this context Orwell's use of the term "Stone Age" is ironic, since only a few years earlier Wells produced a novel, *The Croquet Player*, that presents a very unpromising picture of the lingering influence of modern man's prehistoric heritage. Much of the narrative is the first-person narrator's re-creation of an account given by a Dr. Finchatton about his stay as a medical practitioner in a remote English village shrouded in an atmosphere of malevolence and impending violence. Finchatton's uneasiness deepens after seeing the preserved remains of a Stone Age man in a local museum and hearing the curator's warning that the "cave man, the ancestral ape, the ancestral brute, have returned," and "brooding" over the doctor's subsequent nightmares is an image that becomes the emblem of a primitive past reasserting its savage power— "that infernal palaeolithic skull."[125]

Years before fascism appeared, Hilaire Belloc, in *The Servile State* (1912), predicted the reversion of modern industrial society back to a pre-Christian age of slave labor. As the rule of authoritarian dictators spread and hardened into totalitarian tyrannies seemingly indifferent to international law or human rights, references to a Europe suddenly returning to some form of ethical dark age became commonplace. If for John Sommerfield "Stone Age" refers only to the crude conditions of daily living endured by the men in the trenches around a Madrid besieged by the Franco forces,[126] for Orwell, reviewing Malcolm Muggeridge's satirically pessimistic *The Thirties,* the phrase describes the political and moral backsliding of the age, when "human types supposedly extinct for centuries . . . have suddenly reappeared, not as inmates of lunatic asylums, but as the masters of the world."[127] Bertrand Russell implies that if the revolutionary movement is left in the hands of the Bolsheviks, the result will be Europe's "reversion to barbarism";[128] for Philip Henderson, a Marxist literary critic, it is because of fascism and Nazism that the West is, in the late 1930s, on the edge of a "dark age";[129] and in *The Spirit and Structure of German Fascism,* Brady traces the roots of Nazism back to a barbaric, pre-Romantic Europe.

"That Infernal Palaeolithic Skull"

The neo-barbarian appears first in Orwell's *Burmese Days* as U Po Kyin, whose "quite barbaric" mind is obsessed with the acquisition of power and prestige (8). Like his porcine descendant, Napoleon, in *Animal Farm*, U Po Kyin can establish a relationship with another male only as someone to be used or eliminated as an obstacle to power, and as though seeing himself allegorically reincarnated in Orwell's future fable about the Soviet Union, U Po Kyin seems inspired by a picture of Napoleon before Moscow to formulate a plan to ruin Flory (8, 262). If U Po Kyin's ultimate success as a political manipulator suggests the barbarism at the heart of the colonial system, in Orwell's works dealing with English life there are signs of an ancient past rudely breaking through the crust of modern civilization. In *A Clergyman's Daughter,* tipsy hop pickers making a hullabaloo as they weave down the main street of a village are described as invading "Goths," and the "fearful clamour" of a goose that foils one of Nobby's attempted predations (108, 129) implies a connection between Orwell's natural man and the barbarian marauders who, according to Roman legend, were driven off the Capitoline Hill thanks to the cackling of the sacred geese. In the twentieth century only a thin line divides barbarian from civilized man: supposedly the representatives of provincial respectability, the men in *Animal Farm* angrily invading the animals' cherished homeland are satirically reduced to the level of barbarian intruders in flight from a "flock of geese after them" (36).

At one point in *Burmese Days* the narrator suggests the possibility that the now deceased U Po Kyin might be reincarnated as an unpleasant beast, perhaps as a rat (286). If so, the first mistake made by the inexperienced revolutionaries of *Animal Farm* may have been that of allowing the spirit of U Po Kyin to sour the revolutionary milk—in the form of the rats that the domesticated beasts vote to include in the farm community (9). The Orwellian rat is a demonic being—untameable and potentially destructive. Where there is a rat, there is also a rat hole; and directly or indirectly, for good or ill, holes are associated in Orwell's works with wild energy and anarchic freedom. The rats in

Animal Farm feel safer in their hole than among the animals who have magnanimously—although, ominously, not by a unanimous vote—accepted them as "comrades," and it is because of some other holes—the henhouse "popholes" that Farmer Jones has forgotten to close for the night—that the fowls are able to attend Old Major's talk, which is the philosophical starting point of the animals' eventual self-liberation (3). Orwell's narratives suggest a reason why "modern dictatorships don't . . . leave the loopholes that the old-fashioned despotisms did."[130] In *Coming Up for Air* George Bowling recalls an event portending the outbreak of wild, ungovernable energy that topples Farmer Jones and threatens to throw the pig Napoleon's regime into chaos. Remembering his boyhood practice of plugging the holes of a wasps' nest after pouring turpentine into it so that the grubs could be gathered for fishing bait, George Bowling recollects an instance when the rather cruel activity backfired: "Once something went wrong, the turps missed the hole or something, and when we took the plug out the wasps . . . came out all together with a zoom" (82). Like the rats that, in *Animal Farm,* save their lives by racing back into their holes, the pig Snowball, having incurred Napoleon's hatred, escapes through a "hole in the hedge" (46). And if we are to believe the confessions of three hens that destroyed their own eggs lest they be expropriated by Napoleon, it was through another kind of hole, the aperture of the dream, that the disruptively counterrevolutionary spirit of Snowball entered their minds and thereby moved them to open defiance of the new order (71).

As an instinctive, impulsive reaction to tyranny, this wild energy sets the revolution in motion and introduces the animals to history. However, as the first stage of anarchic revolutionary exuberance begins to harden into authoritarianism, the hole—that open space in the order of things that allows for the appearance of the unexpected and the spontaneous—becomes associated with evil. Sent to the colonial station of Kyauktada to discourage a native uprising, Verrall brands the whole station as a "filthy hole" at finding a Burman sharing his guest bungalow in *Burmese Days* (184). The hole drilled by the enemies of *Animal Farm* is for dynamite to blast away the windmill, itself a breach for the introduction of electric power into the primitive existence of the farm creatures (86).

To the extent that *Animal Farm* alludes to events of the Russian Revolution, the skull of Old Major—first placed on a stump, in a place of honor next to the hoof-and-horn flag and the gun captured at the Battle of the Cowshed, and later, to appease Napoleon's human friends, buried (49, 117)—parallels the actual preservation of Lenin's corpse in Red Square first in a simple vault and later, as though hiding the man's mortal humanity behind a myth of omnipotence or saintliness, in a vast mausoleum. Moreover, the fact that his tomb is close to a spot symbolic of official savagery—the "Place of the Skull," where Ivan the Terrible and Peter the Great had political enemies killed— might have reminded Orwell of the Wellsian paleolithic skull, a warning of the brute energy that could at any time come roaring through a crack in the wall of postrevolutionary order. It is perhaps an awareness of this possibility that causes Orwell's Napoleon, a creature prey to wild impulses behind his front of superhuman calm, to replace the first revolutionary banner, with its emblems of breaking and puncturing, with the unbroken uniformity of the new "plain green flag" (117).

In the porcine rivalry between allegorical representations of the internationalistic Trotsky and the nationalistic Stalin, Snowball embodies an expanding, dynamic view of reality; his social fabric will be permeable to the demonic energies of an ever-changing technology. On the other hand, Napoleon is closer to Orwell's picture of the modern dictator, who—out of an instinctive sense of mass psychology "sounder" than that of the consumption-oriented capitalist democracies— offers his people a national existence of spartan austerity, of hardship and sacrifice.[131] Emblem of the new rational man's open, porous world is the technical drawing Snowball makes on a shed floor—a "complicated mass of cranks and cog-wheels, covering more than half the floor." But what the thinker opens up, the visceral being—the Napoleon who urinates over the drawing—quickly plugs (42–43).

Napoleon's dramatic expulsion of Snowball is the public triumph of a primitive will power and equally primitive distrust and even fear of intellectuality and the defeat of cerebral abstractions. The ouster of Snowball also means the devolution of public life toward a primal simplicity. The driving off of Farmer Jones was the practical starting point of the animal's politicization, and this in turn has introduced them to an unfamiliar existence of complexity and thought since a majority is expected to ratify decisions arrived at by the porcine leaders. Adding to this complexity has been the constant disagreement between the two most influential pigs, Snowball and Napoleon, for whom every issue has become a bone of contention (41). Thus, Snowball's physical disappearance eliminates from the animals' experience the complicating factor of theorizing and the translation of abstract thought into working reality, such as the electricity-driven farm mechanization imagined by Snowball and encoded in his disturbingly abstruse diagrams. Replacing Snowball's unsettling promises of leisure, of empty time, is Napoleon's simple reality of hard work leading to more hard work. In place of the stressful dyadic leadership of the past is a single object of respect, awe, and even veneration. As described in Silone's *The School for Dictators,* which Orwell reviewed in June 1939, the process by which the fascist leader consolidates his power over the people includes the assumption of those types of public identity that are most likely to evoke feelings of dependency deeply rooted in the psyches of his subjects—the leader as the "father who is protector, breadwinner, judge, master, and guide."[132] Similarly, the cult of the leader that Napoleon establishes rests upon mesmerizing displays—the firing of the shotgun, flashy decorations, pageantry—designed to captivate the animals at the deepest emotional level. It is not enough for Napoleon to be just "Father of All Animals": because of the magical power of the title, one's personal power and invulnerability increase with each additional honorific, so Napoleon becomes "Terror of Mankind" and "Protector of the Sheepfold," "Ducklings' Friend," "Friend of the fatherless," "Fountain of happiness"—and even "Lord of the swill-bucket!" (78, 84, 89).

THE DARKENING FUTURE

"We're on the edge of things," cries Montgomery, Moreau's assistant in *The Island of Doctor Moreau,* as the doctor's regime of scientific orderliness starts to crumble. Although written when the war was turning against Germany, *Animal Farm* reflects much the same sense of uncertainty and anxiety about the future as does the more politically aware literature of the previous decade. If the Dorothy Hare of the mid-thirties is only vaguely aware of the "night in the streets ahead of her" (*A Clergyman's Daughter,* 166), her countrymen exposed in the late thirties to an abundance of information and also conflicting views on the contemporary troubles, lived with a deepening sense of foreboding as the European diplomatic situation grew more ominous in the late 1930s. Although Dorothy Hare, having returned to her rural home after her dispiriting stay in modern, commercialized London, seems to feel that she has found a refuge from the great world, in fact, at work in the rectory on pageant costumes illustrative of early English history in *A Clergyman's Daughter* (317), she is one with the madding crowds abroad—preparing for conquest.

During the later 1930s, Orwell's writing tends to stress the influence of the future on an individual's attitudes, so that whatever about the present is considered good, is so in contrast to the evil age bearing down on the present. In *Coming Up for Air,* George Bowling, with hardly a trace of his past to return to, finally decides that a wife in the home, however irritating she may be, is better than a wife in the grave (271), and the larger message implied by this conclusion is that the contemporary British reader should realize that the country he has got, whatever its imperfections, is probably more worthy of his allegiance than the technologically sophisticated barbarism gathering on the other side of the channel. For George Bowling, the physical return to his adult home and life as husband, father, and insurance agent is the start of an interim period, what could be the last stage of his (and his countrymen's) familiar existence before the bombs start falling. This type of situation, the interim period before some strange and menacing future, is common enough in Orwell to be considered a structural motif, as a basic setting. The interim period in which Orwell's faith in a workable working-class socialism was quickened started with his arrival in Spain in December 1936 and extended to around May 1937, until he witnessed the fighting in Barcelona between rival leftist factions—violence that brought to an end a brief period of revolutionary idealism. Also, there is a parallel between Orwell's return to Wallington in July 1937 to think and write about his introduction in Spain to the violence and betrayals of revolutionary activism and the retreat of the humbler beasts in *Animal Farm* to the knoll after witnessing Napoleon's slaughter of fellow animals—where in their limited way they sadly reflect on the gap between utopian dream and dystopian reality (73).

The kind of rural utopia that expresses the animals' deepest pastoral longing involves a relatively static temporal space, an interim period that does not change out of recognition, and a bounded physical space, a known territory with which the animals can identify themselves. The importance of the former condition for the preservation of the beasts' essential animality is made explicit in Old Major's warning against allowing the revolutionary struggle against man to tempt them into taking up his vices and modes of living. At this stage of the animals' story, the implied goal of revolutionary activity is the kind of change that will allow the beasts to more fully experience their basic animality—to close the gap between what nature made them and what man the money-obsessed property owner has done to them. The former condition is symbolically expressed even before the start of Old Major's speech by the "sort of wall" made by the bend of Clover's "great foreleg" around some ducklings (5, 10).

The fragility of the animals' pastoral dream, its vulnerability to the harshly intrusive and disruptive factor of domestic and international power politics, is suggested by images of containment and enclosure that no longer contain and enclose—the stone-and-cement windmill first blown down by a great wind and later blown up by Frederick's dynamite, the acts of sabotage attributed to a Snowball

who is supposedly not stopped by any boundary or wall—the stripped from fruit trees, the milk cans overturned, the eggs bro the "overturned pot of white paint" that Squealer was using to a the commandment prohibiting alcohol consumption, and the o worked Boxer's collapsed lung (59, 66, 86, 91, 99).

Insofar as an interim period has the power to captivate an in vidual, to exhilerate and inspire him, to that extent it offers a con tion of pastoral wholeness and simplicity, a release from the narrati movement of political history toward a problematic, possibly antipa toral future. The "utter intimacy" of a militiaman's handclasp th leads to no further acquaintance, all the visible and tangible signs Barcelona of an achieved, completed revolution (*HC*, 4–5)—thes brief, tonic pastoral moments enable both Orwell the soldier to sur vive the ideologically ambiguous conflict, so full of treachery and be trayals, with his humanity intact, and Orwell the writer to record, in *Homage to Catalonia*, the evils committed in Barcelona without turn- ing the book into a splenetic diatribe.

Nevertheless, for the man of the thirties, a most insistent imper- ative was that demanding a break with the past, with modes of thought and behavior not directed toward the problems and chal- lenges of the future. But the Orwellian sleeper's awakening to the new age is a jolting experience: day begins in a Paris working-class quarter with "furious choking yells from the street"; the "bad omen" herald- ing Orwell's period of grinding servitude in the restaurant in which he has just spent the night is the first thing he sees on awakening—rat on a kitchen table; and the "dark brown thing" before Orwell as h awakens in a London doss house is the too close foot of a tramp i *Down and Out in Paris and London* (5, 105, 131), this final scen being itself unpleasantly close to one of Orwell's more vivid images political repression—the boot stamping on a human face. *A Clerg man's Daughter* begins, as does the toilsome day of its central cha acter, with a jarring sound: the "alarm clock . . . exploded like a bomb" (5). In *Coming Up for Air*, the people George Bowling vie from his hotel window on awakening only deepen his bitterness at

contemporary world: "My enemies," he thinks (249). *Animal Farm* is punctuated with rude awakenings suggesting the characters' unreadiness for the historical role being thrust upon them. No amount of beer can blunt Farmer Jones's consciousness of the "uproar" of the aroused animals below his window, and when next this sleeper wakes it is to the sounds of a rebellion soon "out of . . . control" (12, 16–17). Even though it is exultantly that the beasts awaken on the first morning of their freedom, later the new day will treat them as harshly as it has Jones: on one morning the animals awaken to find their windmill in ruins, and the midnight racket that disrupts their slumber—Squealer's fall from a ladder while altering the wording of the commandment barring alcohol (18, 59, 91)—marks a late stage of the deterioration of revolutionary idealism.

What makes Nazi war aims almost unique in European military history, claims Borkenau, is that they are "unlimited," with warfare being an end in itself (*Totalitarian Enemy*, 171). In *Cauchemar en U.R.S.S.*, a pamphlet Orwell read sometime between its appearance in 1937 and his writing of "Arthur Koestler" in September 1944, Boris Souvarine describes the Soviet Union during the time of the various purge trials as a place of total brutality, of savagery without limits.[133] In the Spain of Orwell's *Homage to Catalonia* communists "go a great deal further" than even the middle-class authorities in persecuting genuine revolutionaries, and since "no one scruples" to conceal ammunition in ambulances, they are commonly fired on (57, 83). In short, the new age to which Orwell was introduced in Spain was marked by a disdain for restraints on behavior. The razing of the forests that upsets the protagonists of *Burmese Days* and *Coming Up for Air* threatens the shaping and protective boundary of pastoral decency; with every stand cut there are fewer obstacles to the cyclonic winds of ideological aggressiveness. In *Burmese Days* it is the ungovernable racial hatred of the Germanophile manager of a timber firm, Ellis, a rage resulting in an attack on a native youth, that triggers the collective rage of the normally peaceful Burmans (242–44). Perhaps fear of the evil consequences of his own felling of a grove of beech trees years

earlier prevented Farmer Jones from selling the timber (65), despite his financial problems. The later handling of the stacked timber by Napoleon, its sale and removal, is a sort of tomb violation that activates a curse: Napoleon's uncharacteristic mental struggle as to which neighboring farmer he should sell conjures up Snowball's invisible and disruptive presence. The atmosphere of disillusionment and betrayal spreading outward from the official villification of Snowball causes the slaughter of supposed saboteurs, and the curse continues until it drives Napoleon, duped into taking worthless banknotes for the timber, into a "rage" to match Ellis's (*AF,* 65–71, 78).

The new age is an uncharted region, maps from the past being useless as guides to the future. Machiavelli's wisdom, derived from the deeds of the ancients, is obsolete in the rapidly changing modern world, claims a dialogist in Silone's *The School for Dictators*—a view endorsed in *Coming Up for Air* in the depiction of the old classicist, Porteous, clearly unable to explain the emergence of totalitarianism. Understanding eludes Porteous's grasp because of his own name, which, slightly altered, is Proteus, god of ever-changing shapes. Having studied Homer at Eton in 1921,[134] Orwell may have bestowed on the young mare Mollie a power similar to that of the Homeric *moly,* an herb that prevents change. With her disappearance from Manor Farm, transforming forces take control as Snowball spins out ever grander visions of technological utopias, and in reaction to his rival's schemes Napoleon is metamorphosed from shrewd leader to tyrant and finally—perhaps—to some sort of humanoid.

The seemingly fated rivalry between Snowball and Napoleon is one instance of a tendency in Orwell's writings for proximity to spark aggressiveness. In *Coming Up for Air* it does not take long for a group of communists sitting together at an antifascist talk to get into their own verbal "dog-fight," a Trotskyist Jew being the main object of attack (177–78). This foreshadows the savage attacks by Napoleon's dogs on unsuspecting comrades at an assembly in *Animal Farm* (71). One reason why the girls in a Paris bistro leave when the males start roughly pawing them (*Down and Out in Paris and London,* 95) and

Mrs. Jones flees when the farmyard uproar begins (17) is fear of the male aggressive impulse, which knows no limits. Shaped like the horn of a water buffalo, Flory's facial discoloration links him to the animal that so frightens Elizabeth Lackersteen (*Burmese Days*, 80); and a real assault is attempted when a drunken Gordon Comstock, casting aside restraint, forces himself on Rosemary (*Keep the Aspidistra Flying*, 166–67).

In choosing to adapt "The Fox"—the English translation of a Silone short story that had appeared in John Lehmann's *New Writing in Europe* (1940)—for a BBC broadcast to India in September 1943, Orwell may well have been influenced by the Italian's fear, as expressed in *The School for Dictators*, that the struggle with fascism could be so "contaminating" as to evoke the "primitive barbarism" from within the psyche of the antifascist.[135] The central character of "The Fox" is Daniele, a pig farmer who lives with his wife and daughters in the Ticino region of Switzerland, across the border from fascist Italy. Although for some time Daniele has been secretly collaborating with Italian antifascists in Switzerland, he is too civilized to turn over to his vengeful Italian associates a fascist agent recuperating at the farmhouse after having been brutally assaulted by his enemies. Daniele's scruples result, however, in the spy's flight with information from Daniele's files that exposes the illegal political activities of the antifascist Italians in Switzerland, and this in turn means the arrest and deportation of these men to Italy—where presumably they will be imprisoned or killed. Earlier, one of these Italians had asserted that "when your enemy is down, smash him," and now an embittered Daniele, having caught a fox that had been raiding his poultry, gives free reign to his own destructive impulses by hacking the predator into a bloody mess.[136] Tragically, in an age of treachery and violence, a civilized man's attempt to remain so only causes greater evil. In these barbaric times even the ancient rule of guest right becomes a deadly folly. The capture of the fox brings out a suppressed, brutal Daniele.

It was Orwell's fear that what happened to Silone's civilized Swiss could occur in England. In view of Orwell's concern regarding the possible growth of a fascist mentality in England, a concern appearing as early as *The Road to Wigan Pier* in 1937 (212), his tendency to focus on the lives and environments of socially and also emotionally marginal types—frustrated, insecure, distrustful, and embittered members of the lower middle class—derived from an interest in the behavior of that social group most likely to yield itself to an authoritarian leader or ideology. The central characters in *A Clergyman's Daughter,* *Keep the Aspidistra Flying,* and *Coming Up for Air* are all prodigal children who are relieved finally to return to a more or less authoritarian domestic situation: Dorothy Hare to the thankless servility of her father's rectory; Gordon Comstock to the sensually repressive shadow of the aspidistra that he insists on placing in his and his wife's apartment right after marriage; and George Bowling to the in-house police state of life with a spouse who keeps him under constant surveillance and subjects him to accusatory interrogations.

The reverse side of submissiveness is control. In the nearly totalitarian atmosphere of Mrs. Creevy's school, Dorothy of *A Clergyman's Daughter* finally becomes a pedagogical tyrant holding her students in "miserable bondage" (264), and in the remembered past and present George Bowling gravitates toward basically submissive types—his first girl friend, Elsie Waters, with whom "you could . . . do what you wanted," and now Porteous, "always ready to have you in and talk at all hours" (*Coming Up for Air,* 121, 182). In the view of the authoritarian mentality, when control fails, the only alternative is decisive and violent action. The sense of his failed life drives Flory to suicide (*Burmese Days,* 281); the sight of sham Tudor houses makes George Bowling, by now the captive of a destructive future, long for a grenade (*Coming Up for Air,* 255).

Fear is an essential ingredient in the witch's brew of totalitarianism, and the idea of it becomes increasingly important in the 1930s. Although man no longer is awed by a now controllable nature, claims Strachey in *The Coming Struggle for Power,* his fear of a socioeconomic system that controls him is as great as ever. Both the "impulse of submission" and the "impulse to command" spring from fear, claims Bertrand Russell,[137] and there is a quality of tragic irony in Boris Souvarine's explanation of the Moscow purge trials as motivated primarily by Stalin's anxiety at the general atmosphere of terroristic violence first generated by the Bolsheviks themselves to consolidate their power.[138] Watching a manager openly berating a shopgirl, who flinches "like a dog that sees the whip," George Bowling in *Coming Up for Air* concludes that both are controlled by the anxiety of the times: "Fear! We swim in it. It's our element" (17–18).

A mode of fear new to the animals' experience may be a key factor in the attempted metamorphosis of creature into comrade. Priming the assembled animals for the revolution to come, Old Major replaces the farm animals' ordinary sense of death—a vague intimation of mortality until, suddenly and unexpectedly, the last-minute terror at the reek of blood and the sight of the knife—with a sustained, long-term, conscious awareness of an inevitable violent death while in Jones's power: "To that horror we all must come—cows, pigs, hens, sheep, everyone" (8). Interestingly, the animals whose domesticated mentality would be most rudely jolted by visions of certain slaughter—"even the horses and the dogs have no better fate," Old Major is quick to add—become the new regime's most ardent supporters. Surely the dogs that Napoleon raises by himself have been taught that for them it is either kill or be killed, and the horses become the pigs' "most faithful disciples," always ready to use persuasively "simple arguments" to propagate the leaders' ideas among the humbler beasts (15). As though mesmerized by the implanted image of his slit throat, Boxer is the most active of the common animals in helping to create the one being, the autocratic master, whose demand for mind-numbing toil can alone blur the mental image of death. More than mere simple-minded fidelity, Boxer's expression of utter confidence in the leader is the blossoming of an authoritarian submissiveness—a dank undergrowth rooted in the soil of anxiety. What Silone's "rank-and-file-Fascist thinks"—"If my leader acts in this manner, it must be right!"[139]—Boxer says aloud. "Napoleon is always right," intones the horse at just the crucial moment when a sign of his disapproval or even doubt might have stalled, if not thwarted, Napoleon's bid for sole power (48). Later, a similar endorsement by Boxer—this regarding Napoleon's claim that Snowball was a traitor from the start (69)—invests the ruler's pronouncements with an aura of infallibility.

The course of violence in *Animal Farm* is along the fracture lines in the barrier between moral sanity and barbarism. Whatever might be Farmer Jones's private motives, he has used his knife on the farm animals in accordance with the economic imperatives of farming, and the later bloody frays between animals and men can be viewed as phases of a larger historical rhythm of revolutionary action and counterrevolutionary reaction. But once the tangible, more or less measurable problems confronting the revolution are dematerialized and demonized into the spirit of Snowball, a sort of Wellsian invisible man, the spirit of violence itself becomes ubiquitous, a bolt of lightning liable to strike anywhere and anytime from a free-floating cloud of suspicion and hysteria. In time, the violence becomes more personal, less definable in terms of a public logic of political ends and means. The corpses piling up in front of Napoleon (71–72) have meaning only as signs of his boundless need for assurances of authority. Moreover, the rumored cruelties of Farmer Frederick—the "terrible stories" of animals starved, flogged, burned alive, and forced into mutilating combat for no other reason than their owner's amusement—ominously hint at something new in the experience of Boxer and the others and something old in Western history. Frederick's atrocities herald the return of a barbaric exultation in cruelty for its own sake.

7

TREES INTO BOOKS, ——
BOOKS INTO TREES
Orwellian Satire and Orwellian Satirists

Farmer Jones's reluctance to sell the timber stacked in the yard for years may be connected with his apparent failure to use his how-to-do-it books to modernize the farm, for these books—the final product of what were once living trees—are reminders of the increasing distance between industrial man and the pastoral world of organic nature. Underscoring the link between tree and tome is the fact that in *Animal Farm* the timber is beech, the Old English word for which is cognate with book. The general significance of this is that the final stage in the human being's development of a civilized identity, the ability to read and write, involves the sacrificial felling of trees—in effect, an assault on nature. Whole forests are "shaved flat," claims Flory in *Burmese Days,* to produce pulp for the London *News of the World* (42). This is the same *News of the World* to which Farmer Jones presumably subscribes in *Animal Farm,* although the use to which he puts it, to cover his face during a boozy nap (16), suggests a vaguely felt need to retransform newsprint back into its original shape as a shady tree. Of course, the leaders of the revolution indulge in no romantic fantasies about trees, and they are quite ready to use their facility with the written word to consolidate their rule. Soon enough Napoleon sells the timber, and Squealer can assume that his reference to the pigs' unending paperwork in the management of the farm—their "enormous labours everyday upon mysterious things called 'files,' 'reports,' 'minutes,' and 'memoranda'" (108)—will be accepted by the other animals as justification for the leaders' material advantages.

Mindful of Ibsen's *The Wild Duck*, Flory issues a warning that "trees avenge themselves" (*Burmese Days*, 42). Orwell might have been reminded of this admonition by a statement in a book about English life he reviewed in August 1943: although widespread literacy has ended the dependency of the common people on the opinions of squire or parson, today people often "read the wrong things"—one of the most disturbing examples of this being the Germans, who "have read about Nazism."[140] Although no friend of the censor, Orwell did believe that certain kinds of literature could adversely affect a reader's moral consciousness, and it was because of his feeling that during the war people's imaginations were susceptible to the imagery of violence that Orwell turned his attention to graphic journalistic reports of war casualties and to the sadomasochistic pulp fiction of James Hadley Chase. During the early and middle forties there was little demand for imaginative writing other than patriotic action-adventure stories; however, it was during this period that Orwell was seriously engaged in defining his role and identity as literary artist in the England of the near future. Orwell would use the book, his writer's imagination and craft, to redeem the felling of the beech by keeping alive a memory of attitudes and values rooted in an earlier pastoral age. Reversing the words of Orlando in *As You Like It*, "these trees shall be my books," Orwell would turn his book into a tree—the tree of the knowledge of pastoral good and political evil.

To the extent that individuals, events, ideas, or institutions are so presented as to appear foolish, immoral, absurd, or grotesque, *Animal Farm* is a satire. From the beginning, Orwell's published fiction (and some of the nonfiction as well) displayed the sharp eye for social types and the tone of moral concern sometimes mounting to indignation that together produce satire. Orwell's targets have ranged from the mental shallowness and snobbishness of the Anglo-Indian in *Burmese Days*, pedagogical authoritarianism and cultural narrowness in *A Clergyman's Daughter*, in *Keep the Aspidistra Flying* the commercialization of language and the emptiness of socialist jargon, and in *Coming Up for Air* the indifference of a society to its preurbanized past. Some of the character types and flaws Orwell holds up for ridicule or censure—the archly superior *memsahib*, the arrogant or unfeeling official, the ineffective social reformer, the prying landlady, the scholar mentally bound to the past—are drawn from life, but, as critics have noted, at times the objects of his satire have appeared earlier in the works of writers Orwell especially admired, such as Swift, Dickens, and Trollope.

More than simply a means by which Orwell developed his craft as a writer, the imitation of recognized models of satiric art was a form of permission—the taking out of a license, as it were—to engage in one of the potentially most damaging and hurtful of artistic occupations. Early in his career as a novelist Orwell was made aware of the problems in store for the social critic: for fear of libel, Orwell's first English publisher, Victor Gollancz, required changes in the scripts of *Burmese Days*, *A Clergyman's Daughter*, and *Keep the Aspidistra Flying* before final acceptance. It was in the increasingly tense political atmosphere of the later 1930s that Orwell was given more direct and personal evidence of the power of the printed word to wound. In a letter to Cyril Connolly, a former schoolmate and lifelong friend, Orwell confided that he had frequently written "rude things" about the writer Stephen Spender, adding that surely Spender "won't mind." Orwell had referred to the left-leaning poet as being one of England's "parlour Bolsheviks" and, his aim lowered below the belt, a symbol of the "pansy Left." Not surprisingly, Spender did mind, and in time Orwell expressed remorse.[141] In a letter of July 1943 Orwell apologized for his rudeness to the pacifist Alex Comfort in a poem in the London *Tribune* critical of Comfort's own satire against writers performing wartime work for the government.[142]

The writer and intellectual who over the years remained Orwell's favorite target of criticism was H. G. Wells—not as the author of scientific romances and comic novels but as the prophet and projector of world utopias. At times, however, Orwell's criticism of the man's ideas shades off into thinly veiled mockery of Wells—short and plumpish—himself. At one point during his wrecking job on the Wellsian mechanized utopia in *The Road to Wigan Pier*, Orwell disdainfully labels this type of future a "paradise of little fat men"; and having sunk his teeth into this rhetorical morsel, Orwell continues to chew on it: Wells supposedly wants a "fat-bellied type of perfectionism," and because of Wells socialism is now stigmatized by a "fat-bellied, godless" idea of progress (193, 203, 210, 218). There is more than a hint of Wells the public lecturer with his high-pitched voice (and of Wells the author of *All Aboard for Ararat*, with its prophecy that in the postwar utopian world society only one system of sociopolitical ideas will be permitted) in Napoleon's porcine mouthpiece and apologist—the "small fat . . . Squealer, with . . . round cheeks, twinkling eyes, and a shrill voice" (14). Moses the raven, with his promises of a "Sugarcandy Mountain" awaiting the farm animals (97), can be seen as a reincarnation of "Philip Raven," the fictional scholar whose posthumous papers are the basis of H. G. Wells's prophetic history in his 1933 *The Shape of Things to Come*—a fictionalized history of the origin, development, and establishment of an enlightened world state. The description of Orwell's raven "croaking loudly" as he closely follows Mrs. Jones in her escape from the farm (17) may allude to another aspect of Wells's career—his reputation for compulsive womanizing, even with associates' wives.

Although presumably no lasting harm resulted from an occasional barb at this or that public figure, it seems that at times Orwell is revelling in the power of verbal abuse that he once termed "base" in reference to Thomas Carlyle, a "master of belittlement."[143] It is hard not to suspect that Orwell's baiting of middle-class British socialism in *The Road to Wigan Pier*—he calls it an organization of "cranks" appealing to "every fruit-juice drinker, nudist, sandal-wearer, sex-

maniac . . . pacifist and feminist" in the country (174)—is done more
in combative delight than in sorrow. And there may be more than a
chance similarity between the title character of *Gulliver's Travels*—
which Orwell read just before his eighth birthday and repeatedly
thereafter[144]—who, by the end of his adventures, was unable to tolerate the physical presence of fellow-Englishmen, and the Orwell who
once claimed to be so "sick" of the times that on occasion he felt
"almost impelled to stop at a corner and start calling down curses
from Heaven like Jeremiah or Ezra."[145]

Most of Orwell's novels of the 1930s have characters (often the
protagonists) whose dissatisfactions with the world around them
reach such extremes of bitterness that it is difficult to distinguish the
satiric persona, the figure of outraged virtue, from the malcontent, a
traditional butt of satire. These are characters to whom might be applied Orwell's explanation for Carlyle's spitefulness—the "spleen of
the *unconscious* egoist."[146] Although in *Burmese Days* a reader is in-
clined to accept as authoritative and valid the brief anti-imperialist
essays slipped into the narrative as Flory's set speeches or as summa-
ries of his thinking, the nature of his function as central character is
made problematic by the distorting effect of his emotional condition.
So "poisoned" is he by an "ever bitterer hatred" of colonial life that,
as the omniscient narrator reveals to be Flory's own realization, his
judgments are somewhat "septic" and at times unfair (43, 68). Chronically resentful at his surroundings and always ready to vent his dis-
pleasure, the Orwellian social critic and moralist lives in a condition
of almost total isolation. Either indifferent to or disdainful of the
Knype Hill groups whose religious preferences do not exactly conform
to his own narrow practice, Dorothy Hare's father has managed to
alienate just about everyone in his parish (*A Clergyman's Daughter*,
23), and in *Keep the Aspidistra Flying*, Gordon Comstock's repeatedly
proclaimed loathing for the modern city and its values either causes
or serves as an excuse for his social descent into a nearly reclusive
existence.

Perhaps the most insistent issue with which Orwell had to deal in
determining the nature of his critical intention in *Animal Farm*—that

is, the extent, intensity, and direction of the satire—was the question of the relationship between the writer's social responsibility during a period of national crisis and the artist's need to give expression to the promptings of his imagination. Complicating this issue was Orwell's increasing awareness that the two imperatives might be not simply different but opposed. Even before Orwell's reading of Silone's *The School for Dictators,* which unearths a frustrated artistic drive as an important factor in the careers of Hitler and Mussolini, a number of Orwellian characters combine rudimentary signs of an artistic bent with traces of an authoritarian mentality. In *Burmese Days* it is as the virtuoso of the poison pen that U Po Kyin boasts to his wife of the anonymous letters he has sent to various white officials to undermine his inoffensive rival, Dr. Veriswami, in the colonial station: "every one of them a masterpiece," he insists (135). Among the English at the station it is Ellis, rabidly determined to maintain an absolute distinction between white-skinned masters and dark-skinned subjects, who is making a name for himself in two oral genres—as a "genuinely witty" teller of obscene jokes and as creator of scandalous rumors that eventually develop into a "species of saga" (27, 199). Even Dorothy Hare, the wanderer whose general innocence and relative lack of ethical or sociological preconceptions fit her for the role of naive persona through whom the reader can perceive the gap between England's rural past and its commercialized present, is affected. The identity from which Dorothy escapes physically and mentally in her flight from the rectory is that of amateur artist at work on paper costumes for a British historical pageant, and the particular objects on which she is toiling when she suddenly flees and which await her attention when she returns are "jackboots" (*A Clergyman's Daughter,* 95, 313)—meant for Oliver Cromwell but emblematic of the spirit of militant fascism about to force its way into the English consciousness. Spontaneously welling up in the mind of the poet Gordon Comstock, embittered by the indifference of the London reading public and literary coteries, are images of massive destruction raining down on the city in *Keep the Aspidistra Flying* (16–17).

Indicative of Orwell's accelerating concern with the artistic imagination in an age of atavistic political emotions is the number of thoughtful literary essays and review articles that appeared in the forties—from "Charles Dickens" in 1940 to "Politics vs. Literature: an Examination of *Gulliver's Travels*" in 1946. Also, as talks producer in the Indian Section of the BBC's Eastern Service in the early 1940s, Orwell wrote several scripts dealing with satire and satirists. In one of them Orwell, here a defender of material progress interviewing a skeptical Jonathan Swift, raises the point that the radically reductive satiric vision expressed by *Gulliver's Travels* (assumed by Orwell to represent Swift's own attitude) is not only false but also sinister in that it so denigrates ordinary human life as to justify a suppressive political system similar to Nazism—a charge that leaves Orwell's Swift unfazed. At the end, with Swift's final judgment on mankind—his reciting of a misanthropic Gulliver's last words—fading away in the background, the Orwellian interviewer states that even though Swift's insights are "penetrating," he was unable to "see what the simplest person sees, that life is worth living and human beings . . . are mostly decent." But, Orwell concludes, without such a distorted view of human life Swift probably could not have written *Gulliver's Travels*.[147]

In the questionable belief that the fictional character's soured view of humanity must reflect the outlook of the author, Orwell here sets forth the terms of a dilemma facing him as a serious writer and social critic. To the extent that he felt committed to direct his writing at the follies and evils of the period, his satire could be Horatian in being based on the optimistic assumption that people, although erring, are on the whole good-willed, reasonable, and thus corrigible. Modernized, the Horatian satirist would be socially and politically responsible, using his art to improve society and thus to enhance the dignity of its members. At the other extreme, however, is Juvenalian satire. Its reality is a potentially boundless world of evil ranging from criminality to madness and drawing the satirist-explorer into the depths of the perverse and the grotesque. This satirist is closer to the Swift of the BBC program—the radical pessimist whose art could pass beyond the exposure of men's absurdities and inequities to a nihilistically reductive assault on humanity itself. It is at this point, the Orwellian interviewer implies, that satirist and Nazi merge.

The dangers of an uncontrolled satiric impulse are indicated in Orwell's earlier works. In *A Clergyman's Daughter* the accounts of actual or imagined misbehavior by Mrs. Semprill, the hypocritically moralistic scandalmonger, go beyond the merely "dirty" into the "monstrous" (53). In *Burmese Days* the satirist's aggressiveness turns to violence as Ellis passes beyond vituperative outbursts against natives showing signs of an egalitarian attitude to a physical assault, and the inward-turned aggressiveness of another satirist-malcontent, Flory, leads to his suicide. The general biliousness of the misanthropic protagonist of *Keep the Aspidistra Flying* greases his descent into a subworld of squalor and nihilism.

WRITING FOR THE COMMON MAN

Too deep a descent into the consciousness of evil can turn Juvenalian outrage into fascination, satirist into celebrant. The fact that in "Prophecies of Fascism," a review of Jack London's *The Iron Heel*, Orwell could appreciate the relationship between the political prescience of the novel and the "streak of savagery" within its author[148] did not lessen his uneasiness in the 1940s at the direction of contemporary literature toward extremes of violence and morbidity. In the essay "Raffles and Miss Blandish" Orwell leaves little doubt as to his feelings in shifting the focus of the essay away from E. W. Hornung's *Raffles* novels, presented as examples of the descriptively and thematically restrained crime fiction of an earlier England, to the contemporary no-holds-barred crime fiction of James Hadley Chase—a "header into the cesspool" of fascist and sadomasochistic fantasy.[149] For a BBC broadcast of 9 October 1942 Orwell wrote the first installment of a five-part "Story by Five Authors," Orwell's contribution being an introductory episode suggesting the destructive power of the imagination freed from moral constraints. Taking refuge one night in a bombed house during an air raid on London in 1940, Gilbert Moss discovers the unconscious form of Charles Coburn, a wealthy aristocrat and a decade or so earlier an acquaintance of Moss. Moss's initial reaction is a sharpened awareness of his hatred toward the wealthy in general; then memory calls up some unspecified "injury" that Coburn had once done him. At this point, however, memory seems to give way to imagination: unable to recall ever having actually seen the descriptively detailed "vision" he now has of a London street scene of the 1920s, with its atmosphere of moneyed snobbishness, Moss thinks that he may have created a mental symbol of all that he has hated. Gripping a piece of wood at the same moment that his own consciousness is gripped by imagery conjured up from an area of the mind where the power of memory and of imagination are one, Moss (symbolic as an Old English word for swamp) becomes a Stone Age avenger: "he ... gripped his club," the reader is informed "ready for a blow that would settle his enemy once and for all."[150] Boring down into the psychological and historical past, the creative memory opens a hole for the explosive power of primitive rage.

The extent to which by the early forties Orwell had become concerned with controlling the aggressive effects of his own powers as a literary artist is indicated by his essay on Salvador Dali, "Benefit of Clergy: Some Notes on Salvador Dali" (written but not published in June 1944), and the BBC broadcasts "Bernard Shaw" (22 January 1943) and "Lady Windermere's Fan, a Commentary," on Oscar Wilde (21 November 1943). The central argument of the broadcasts is that so effective was the debunking of Victorian taboos by these satirists, representatives of advanced thinking at the turn of the century, that now, at mid-century, there are no conventions in English life that need to be satirized.[151] The implication of this curious conclusion is that Orwell should either abandon the role of satirist or find some other target. In the following year, in the essay on Dali written soon after the completion of Animal Farm, Orwell all but announced his own allegiance as intellectual and artist to the attitudes and values of the common man—a term that by this time included the middle class as well as workers—by tracing the life-negating perversity of the Spaniard's art to a need not to appear "commonplace." Reprehensible, too, are Dali's apologists who claim for the artist an exemption from the "moral laws . . . binding on ordinary people."[152]

The attack on Dali (perhaps the parting shot in Orwell's private Spanish Civil War) represents, then, the full development of a literary personality heralded as early as his 23 July 1936 review of Cyril Connolly's novel about upper-class decadence, *The Rock Pool*, in which Orwell chided the author for not dealing with "ordinary people,"[153] and displayed also in the two cheers given for "bourgeois democracy" in 1941 because the "common people" equate it with "honesty and common decency."[154] In identifying with the very broad majority referred to as the "common people," Orwell was suppressing his earlier identity as satirist of the middle classes.

A telling example of this change is the long essay "The English People," which, commissioned by Collins Publishers in September 1943 and written the following spring, must have been on Orwell's mind as he was writing *Animal Farm*. It seems likely that the fair-minded foreign observer through whose eyes the essayist is describing the basic realities of English thought and behavior is a prodigal Orwell—who returned to his cultural home twice from India, once from France, and once from Spain, like Dorothy Hare and George Bowling returning to their familial homes, and who now, with his impulse to rage at society like a Jeremiah or Ezra suppressed, stands becalmed on the bedrock of English qualities. The British abhorrence of bullying and violence, their refusal to regard might as right and willingness to defend the weak, the enjoyment of commonplace pleasures without tending toward hedonistic excess, the political behavior free of ideological animosity and marked by self-control and moderation—these traits are not only a national profile but also a stage in a line of argument leading to the conclusion that the British nation has a future mission that it should now be preparing itself for—to present itself to the postwar world of big power rivalries as a force for political and ideological restraint and as the exemplar of a humane and workable democracy.[155]

The satire in *Animal Farm* has two important aims—both based on the related norms of limitation and moderation. First, *Animal Farm* exposes and criticizes extremist political attitudes as dangerous. On the one hand, it satirizes the mentality of the utopian revolutionary—the belief that through the conscious effort of a ruling elite a society can be suddenly severed from its past and fashioned into a new, rational system—by showing that the Apollonian dream of technological progress and reason's rule inevitably evokes the Dionysiac reaction of barbaric unreason. Implicit in Snowball's vision of high-technology modernization is the extirpation of the animals' recent agricultural identity as domesticated creatures and—if Boxer's goal of improving his mind is any indication (100), their eventual transformation into Swiftian Houyhnhnms. Instead, Snowball's futuristic incantations conjure up a Stone Age Yahoo—the power-hungry and pleasure-loving Napoleon.

The other extreme attitude being satirically rejected is the nihilistic disbelief in any kind of progress resulting from political activism. Although neither biological nor industrial reality has kept pace with theory—the "expected" population explosion on the farm and its envisioned electrification—life is in some respects better. Toward the end of the narrative it appears that the animal community has insured its physical survival—the most basic of needs—by a noticeable increase in its number, and limited improvements on the original farm, such as the erection of a windmill for the traditional purpose of milling corn for profit, has made the farm a going concern from which the still toiling animals can at least derive a sense of collective achievement (106–10).

The other general aim of *Animal Farm* as satire is to offer itself as an example of temperate, responsible criticism—in no way a rancorous verbal assault. If the ancient Greek's depiction of gods and heroes in a state of sexual erection is a classic form of satiric reduction in showing that figures of mythic or tragic grandeur are basically the same as other men and even animals,[156] then the more aggressive satirist might go beyond reductive obscenity to reductive mutilation to turn hero into eunuch. As though to check the momentum of his own harshly moralistic excoriation of Salvador Dali in "Benefit of Clergy," Orwell turns on those antiartistic types whose opposition to the great writers of twentieth-century modernism he characterizes as an attempt "to castrate the past."[157] In *Animal Farm* the castration knives thrown down the well just after the animals' initial revolt (18) suggest that Orwell's satire will be no iconoclastic wrecking job on a Stalinist Russia whose people had been suffering so cruelly from the war and whose soldiers, under Stalin's leadership, were locked in desperate combat with the German invader even as *Animal Farm* was being written. That Orwell's assault is primarily on an idea, the extremist fantasy of technological utopianism devoid of hard work, and less a living creature, the commander in chief, is demonstrated during the most dramatic moment of Farmer Frederick's attack on the farm—the juxtaposition of the dynamited (symbolically castrated) windmill and the figure of Napoleon alone standing unbowed (86). And despite Orwell's fascination with *Gulliver's Travels,* it is a sign of his attempt to draw back from the Swiftian revulsion at the flesh—a disgust that, as Orwell later noted in "Politics vs. Literature: An Examination of *Gulliver's Travels,*" could extend to political behavior[158]—toward a more balanced and positive view of life that *Animal Farm,* despite its violence, has few references to distasteful physical realities, and those few are appropriate to the events of the narrative. The difference extends to the bad smell—a feature common to the writings of both men. If ever Orwell had an opportunity to indulge a penchant for the reek it was with a farmyard setting. In fact, however, olfactory details (as with sensory details in general) are rare in *Animal Farm*. Of the five references to smells or the act of smelling (11, 19, 61, 84, 95), none are sensorily displeasing in themselves, three are pleasant, and the other two—Napoleon's claim to have detected the banished Snowball's scent and Boxer's sniffing at the banknotes from a timber sale—are negative only in terms of plot context. For the Orwell of *Animal Farm,* the bad odor was in bad odor.

Moreover, in *Animal Farm* the most likely successor to Orwell's previous social critics and the most temperamentally Swiftian of the animals is the donkey, Benjamin—the "worst tempered" of the beasts, the "oldest," and the most prone to the "cynical remark" (4). But unlike Orwell's malcontents, whose satiric volubility reveals as much about their own neuroses as about the world's failings, Ben is taciturn, and his claim that he knows of nothing "to laugh at" (5) suggests an aversion to Swiftian derisiveness. And as well as being a mark of Orwell's rejection of what he considered to be Swift's misanthropy, the long-lived, seemingly imperishable Ben may signify Orwell's refusal to allow satiric outrage to degenerate into the life-denying perversity he found in the art of Dali. One of the more grotesque symbols of Dali's perversity in *The Secret Life of Salvador Dali*—the 1942 Dial Press edition of which Orwell read sometime before his mentioning of this fact in the 10 March 1944 "As I Please" essay[159] and thus possibly before or during the composition of *Animal Farm*—is the eyeless, putrefying corpse of a dead donkey.[160]

Finally, the moderateness of Orwell's satire is reinforced by a treatment of time that encourages the reader's sympathetic understanding of the whole revolutionary experiment from its spontaneous and joyous beginnings to its ambiguous condition on the final page. A basic strategy of scathing social satire is to dehistoricize the society or the specific sociopolitical phenomena being exposed to ridicule and condemnation. Once removed from its historical context, stripped of all the material and cultural determinants responsible for its existence, a practice or institution stands like King Lear's "poor naked wretches" exposed to the "pitiless storm" of the satirist's lashings. The fact that of all Orwell's separately published narratives, *Animal Farm*, the shortest in length, contains the longest time span between the first event of the narrated present and the last—a period of time greater than the four calendar years referred to by the narrator—allows the presentation of factors that to some extent implicitly explain and thus mitigate the follies and abuses of the revolution. Without a past to account for his present behavior, Don Quixote's deeds would be mere zaniness; with a past, the years spent poring over chivalric romances, his follies become humanly understandable, even noble. In *Animal*

Farm the past that jolts the creatures from the timeless present of the animal condition into the manic state of historical consciousness is a quick, magically transformative moment—the past that Old Major springs on the other beasts during his nocturnal talk. And as mentioned in chapter 2 regarding Boxer's behavior, the fact that this introjected consciousness involves the vivid awareness of suffering and bloodshed—the animals being a collective sacrifice on the altar of profit—invests the narrative with an element of pathos that deepens satiric red into a tragic purple. This is not to say that a satiric code is not operant: Napoleon is the conniving, knavish master of Juvenalian satire; Squealer is still the satiric servant all too willing to carry out his master's evil schemes, as is shown by his glibly pseudoscientific justification for the brain-working pigs' hogging of the milk and apple rations (30); and the subject beasts remain gulls. Nevertheless, the nagging thought that Jones could return—not only Jones the individual at the terrifying center of the animals' recently acquired historical consciousness but also countless Jones types armed with noose and knife—encourages the writer and the reader alike to balance satiric mockery with sympathy.

ANIMAL FARM AS ALLEGORICAL FABLE

For the last several centuries readers have regarded allegory as artificial and as foreign to their conception of imaginative literature as the allegory of the playwright Sheridan's Mrs. Malaprop—a creature to be found on the banks of the Nile. And the adult reader's attitude toward the fable has been only slightly more indulgent, it being regarded as a painless form of moral or prudential instruction for the young. The modern reader's lack of enthusiasm for allegory—ordinarily defined as a series of images metaphorically evoking within the reader's mind a corresponding structure of ideas—derives from the feeling that allegorical thinking is unimaginative, its imagery referring either to concepts too abstract and rationalistic to excite the emotions or to figures and events so specific or so historically remote as to interest only scholars. And the plotting of the fable, a form of allegory, is regarded as too rigidly controlled to stamp out a message too obvious or too simplistic to engage the interest of readers attuned to the irony, obliqueness, and ambiguities of modern literature.

Even though Orwell never wrote at length on allegory, scattered remarks on individual allegories suggest a qualified acceptance of it. In a spring 1930 review of Lewis Mumford's *Herman Melville*, Orwell implies that allegory is that which remains after a work has been excessively interpreted—an activity he compares to "eating an apple for the pips."[161] However, a book that he generally praised in a review appearing in the month before he began *Animal Farm*, Michael Foot's fictional *The Trial of Mussolini*, Orwell refers to as an "allegory."[162] In "Arthur Koestler," written sometime in the same year that *Animal Farm* was completed, Orwell criticizes the novel *Spartacus* not because it is an allegory of modern politics but because Koestler failed to elaborate on the basis of the allegorical form.[163]

In *Homage to Catalonia* Orwell recalls a scene in a Spanish train station—the sight of a train full of wounded soldiers waving their crutches and bandaged hands encouragingly to a trainload of foreign volunteers headed for the front. "It was like an allegorical picture of war," Orwell wrote, "the trainload of fresh men gliding proudly up the line, the maimed men sliding [sic] slowly down, and all the while the guns on the open trucks making one's heart leap as guns always do" (192). The author of *Animal Farm* was to some extent a product of the social and cultural conditions of the 1930s, and this passage microcosmically images a prevalent response to the Spanish Civil War and one of the strongest literary impulses of the decade—the need to allegorize. For outsiders the Spanish conflict took on the character of an allegorical struggle (the battle being a standard feature of allegory) between such vast abstractions as Democracy and Fascism, Left and Right, Christianity and Secularism. And surely some foreigners were drawn to what they saw as another allegorical archetype—the journey-quest as rite of passage from political innocence to political worldliness. Mrs. Malaprop's allegories had left the banks of the Nile and were now hungrily teeming the banks of the Ebro and the Thames.

It is fair to claim that the bulk of the literature representative of the social and political concerns of imaginative writers in the 1930s bore the impress of allegorical thinking—often in the form of fable, parable, or morality. Victor, the Anglican parish schoolmaster in *A Clergyman's Daughter,* knows what he is about in proposing, to the dismay of a weary Dorothy, another historical pageant: with its penchant for ritualized displays of tradition, the English public is especially receptive to the procession—one of the standard mediums of allegory. If during her subsequent wanderings in Kent and London Dorothy loses her belief in God, the fervor with which, after her adventures, she once more works on this pageant of British history—"we must make that pageant a success!" (320)—implies an awakened determination to replace the lost religious faith with a sense of her Englishness—an increasingly important theme in Orwell's writings. In fact, a close look at Orwell's longer narratives—ordinarily thought of as predominantly realistic with a documentarylike focus on specific, concrete details—reveals not only a number of allegorical figures and vignettes but also a general pull in the direction of the allegorical fable.

The Malvern Hills of the prologue to William Langland's fourteenth-century allegory, *Piers the Plowman,* from which a dreaming Piers looks down on the "fair field full of . . . men . . . on their worldly business,"[164] reappears in the starkly realistic presentation of parish life at Knype Hill, from which an often benumbed Dorothy starts out, in a fugue condition, on a journey through an England given over to "worldly business." Harrowed from the hell of Mrs. Creevy's authoritarian and humiliating control, Dorothy returns to Knype Hill where—like a modern, faithless Piers Plowperson working her own half-acre—she toils away at the allegorical pageant. In *Homage to Catalonia* the Orwell who had to flee with his wife from the manhunts and purges and imprisonments going on in Barcelona may be a twentieth-century Lot escaping from a doomed contemporary Sodom, although the title of an autumn 1942 essay expressing an unshakable concern with the ideological issues of that conflict, "Looking Back on the Spanish Civil War,"[165] suggests that this fascination with politics might be turning him into Lot's wife—changed into a pillar of salt for looking back at the city of sin.

As an allegorical warning against the wartime Soviet ally, *Animal Farm* is in the spirit of John Gay's "The Gardener and the Hog" (1727), a fable in which a gardener's pet hog, drunk from ale (like Orwell's Napoleon), tramples down the garden and then slashes the too trusting youth's leg—the moral being that he "who cherishes a brutal mate / Shall mourn the folly soon or late."[166] A good example of what Orwell was up against was a directive from the British Ministry of Information to Orwell and other BBC news broadcasters during the war. Headed "Arguments to counter the ideological fear of 'Bolshevism,'" the directive's gist is that the BBC should play up the purported virtues of the Soviet Union—its scientific and cultural advances, its encouragement of individual initiative and ownership of private property, and its tolerance toward religion and rejection of international revolutionary activity, as well as the unlikelihood of its gaining control of Europe—while branding any negative views as Nazi propaganda.[167a] Given Orwell's interest in keeping British socialism free of authoritarian foreign influences, and the fact that by 1945 a general election would have to take place in England (an election that might put in power the only major party receptive to socialist programs, Labor), it is understandable that "The Freedom of the Press"— an essay written in 1944 or 1945 as an introduction to *Animal Farm* but in fact not published with it—would define the writer's liberty as the "right to tell people what they do not want to hear."[167b] Orwell's message to Labor was to accept the Fabian horse within the gates but to make sure it concealed no Stalinist shock troops.

Not surprisingly, two important themes conveyed through the allegory are incognizance, a lack of information or awareness, and the perfidy of associates. Not only are the important truths not known, often both beast and man attempt to block them from consciousness. Stupefied with alcohol, Farmer Jones can sink into the depths of sleep

unmindful of his mate's snoring and the implicit commentary the
sound is making on the marriage, and Napoleon's drunken condition
makes it easier for him to don Jones's hat (89–90) without having to
face the full implications of this action in relation to his animal identity. The roar of the shotgun that temporarily restores Jones's farmyard
world to its normal identity is a parallel to the "tremendous bleeting"
of the sheep that quashes rational debate regarding Snowball's expulsion (12, 47). The conscious and willing assumption of a political,
revolutionary identity is either cause or effect of the mark of Cain
branded into the leaders' behavior: one look at Snowball's engineering
plans is enough to turn Napoleon's recent comrade-in-arms into a rival
that must be destroyed; Napoleon has no qualms about selling timber
to Frederick, whom the animals loathe above all other human beings
for his sadism—and who shamelessly uses the deal to defraud Napoleon (80–84); reasonably expecting to be rewarded for his labors with
a leisurely retirement, old Boxer is sold to the horse-slaughterer; and
that betrayal is becoming the norm is indicated by the cheating at
cards during the pigs' and human beings' unity banquet (80–84, 101,
118).

An allegorical view of reality—the thing said or displayed really
meaning something else—suited the Marxist-oriented social criticism
of the 1930s, which was indefatigable in pointing out the economically self-serving motives underlying the surface features of modern
bourgeois society. One form of allegory is the masque, a spectacle with
masked participants, and by the 1940s Orwell was busy exposing
what he considered the questionable motives behind the mask of leftist
politics. There is something similar to a dropped mask in the *r* that
when removed from the "dictatorship" supposedly planned by middle-
class socialist "prigs" in *The Road to Wigan Pier* (183), becomes the
later dictatorship of pigs. The reader of Orwell's allegory can engage
in an unmasking too: by mentally dropping the *r* from a word to
which attention is called—the incorrectly spelled "freind" and the correct "friend" of the commandment distinguishing the four-legged comrade from the two-legged enemy in *Animal Farm* (21)—we can

anticipate the metamorphosis of friend into fiend and freind into the German cognate, *Feind* (foe).

In James Burnham's *The Machiavellians* (1943; reviewed by Orwell in January 1944) leftist agitation for widespread democracy and mass suffrage are unmasked as a strategy for the installation of an anti-individualistic Bonapartism (after Napoleon Bonaparte), with one person or small group taking complete control of the society. In a quite similar vein, in *Animal Farm* Orwell is exposing the selfish power-hunger of the few behind a collectivist rhetoric used to gull the many. And in at least two ways Orwell's allegorical exposure is also an exposure of allegory. Because the surface fiction tends to be considered of lesser importance than the implied meaning, allegory is inherently hierarchical, and the insistence on a dominant meaning makes it an authoritarian mode.[168] Thus it is a spokesman of the ruling elite, the smooth-talking Squealer, who delights in his task of providing the ideologically correct—that is, porcine—interpretation of such matters as the leaders' enjoyment of special privileges, the farm's setbacks and failures, and even Boxer's sordid death. Also, since to Orwell so much of the public pageantry surrounding Stalin was itself an allegorical display of a largely nonexistent socialism, *Animal Farm* can be seen as allegory satirizing allegory.

If allegory tends to subordinate narrative to thesis, the structure of allegory, its dualistic form, can be emphasized to restore a balance between fictional events and conceptual message. In *Animal Farm* there are signs of a balance struck between satiric devices allegorically martialed to expose and assault a dangerous political myth and collateral apolitical elements—the latter akin to the "solid objects and useless scraps of information" that as Orwell claims in "Why I Write," have a place in literature.[169] Orwell's model in respect to this is Charles Dickens, whose literary trademark was, as Orwell italicizes in "Charles Dickens," the *"unnecessary detail"*—"picturesque details" that may be irrelevant to the plot but which "were too good to be left out."[170] (*CEJL*, 1:450, 454). Dickens's literary imagination (and that of premodern writers in general, in Orwell's view) was unhampered by any conscious ideology. Paradoxically, the duality of *Animal Farm*—politically topical elements existing alongside the seemingly gratuitous—owes something to Orwell's reading of certain more or less political works in the late thirties and early forties. These are Winwood Reade's *The Martyrdom of Man* (1872), Peter F. Drucker's *The Future of Industrial Man* (1942), James Burnham's *The Machiavellians,* and probably Arthur Koestler's "The Yogi and the Commissar" (first published in 1942 in *Horizon*) with whose works Orwell, Koestler's friend, was familiar. Common to the thinking of these men was skepticism regarding the proclaimed benefits of extremist revolutionary activism. The Victorian Reade denied the assumption of the revolutionary and the utopianist that human nature could be radically altered in a short period of time,[171] and Koestler's essay formulates a law of revolutions that impels them toward self-defeating extremes.[172] Koestler's view of progressivist aspirations as forking into two antithetical modes—that of the commissar intent on effecting external social change versus the yogi's inward focus on personal moral development (3–4)—suggests the concept of the "mixed society" in Burnham and Drucker, which Orwell described as a "system of checks and balances" in society that would make it "impossible for any one section of the community to become all-powerful."[173]

Although Orwell was at times critical of Burnham, *The Machiavellians* did leave its imprint on *Animal Farm*. Burnham's exposition of Machiavelli's thought and that of later Machiavellians emphasizes ideas that could serve as a gloss on *Animal Farm*—the inevitable rise to power of a capable and organized elite, that elite's rationalizing of its position by some idealistic or mythic formula that could eventually become a socially cohesive tradition, and a driving will to power turning the leader into a Bonapartist embodiment of the popular will (90–91, 99–100, 161). As the subtitle of Burnham's book indicates, the Machiavellian thinkers are defenders of freedom in that they stressed the importance of social forces to check the potentially totalitarian monopolization of power by one man or a single group (70, 109–12). That *Animal Farm* is dramatizing Burnham's Machiavellian view of an uneasy tension between uniformity and pluralism is suggested by references early in the narrative to a fox and the Red Lion—both animals also referred to by Burnham as emblems of the Machiavellian ruler.

Animal Farm embodies a double vision of society—society as a stage or arena for the display of an elite group's or a dominant individual's increasingly extreme self-regarding behavior and, on the other hand, as a commonplace setting for the muted celebration of communal values. In Animal Farm some of the world, but not all, is a stage, and the ascendancy of the porcine leaders owes as much to their flair for the dramatic, their seemingly innate theatricality, as to their braininess. The pigs are drawn to the stage and its tricks. Speaking from a raised platform, Old Major holds the attention of his late-night audience by first mentioning the "strange dream" that the animals have assembled to hear about and then delaying an account of it until after having lectured his sleepy listeners into a state of suggestibility. "Skipping from side to side and whisking his tail" while explaining away porcine selfishness as selfless statesmanship (30–31), Squealer is perfecting a propagandistic song-and-dance act. It is fair to assume that in Snowball's mind the most delightful feature of the leisure society he envisions is the free time the other animals will have to give ear to his "brilliant speeches" (41). Napoleon is the most Machiavellian pig's name, and histrionics—not just history—is his game: an Eisenstein's Ivan the Terrible in his periods of brooding bursting into fits of rage (the film biography having appeared in 1942), the bemedalled and strutting Napoleon is also the pompous ruler of Chaplin's The Great Dictator (1940). And the animals seem destined for certain roles and fates by the names given them by Farmer Jones or some other human being. Named Boxer, what else could an Edwardian draft horse expect out of life but some form of martyrdom? Some obscure martial passion must have been stirred into life by the change of name from "the Willingdon Beauty" to "Old Major"; the curious career of Snowball—the cyclic expansion and contraction of his real or imaginary power—is there freeze dried in his name; and the English farmer who would name one vigorous young boar Napoleon without raising another one named the Duke of Wellington was asking for trouble. On a flyleaf of Orwell's copy of *The Future of Industrial Man* is a page reference to a passage in Drucker's book defining the range of meaningful sociopolitical freedom, and after the page reference is the following comment (in what appears to be Orwell's hand): "Man is not only his brother's keeper, he is his brother's brother." Rather than a sentimental tautology, this statement, with its allusion to the stormy relationships of biblical brothers, calls attention to what may be the central motif of *Animal Farm* as political commentary—the inevitable transformation of association into enmity. Entry into political history is a journeying into a Hobbesian state of nature ruled by rivalry, distrust, and betrayal. But if this were all there were to *Animal Farm*, it would be for writer and for reader a "header into the cesspool" of political pornography. Instead, however, it is a bipolar narrative, the literary counterpart of a balanced society, in which political allegory, although important, is held in check by other modes of experience.

The Animal as Literary Beast of Burden

A basic satiric assumption about animals is that they are suitable devices for presenting man as ridiculous or brutal, and Orwell's narratives of the early thirties are studded with examples of animal imagery used by Orwell and his characters for purposes of satiric reduction. However, toward the end of the decade, when the harsh spotlight of Orwell's reductive satire was tending to shade off into the deeper tones of a philosophical pessimism mixed with compassion, his animal imagery came to be used as a means of evoking for his flawed and vulnerable human characters some of the positive feelings spontaneously and unconditionally awakened in us by animals. Any conclusions regarding the use of animal imagery in *Animal Farm* for debunking and reductive purposes should take into account not only Orwell's deepening interest in animals in their own right in the later thirties (feelings owing in part to his farming activities at Wallington) but also the expanded meanings associated with animal imagery. In the long essay "The Lion and the Unicorn: Socialism and the English Genius," written in 1941, one of the darkest periods of British history, Orwell's faith in the nation's ability to survive is metaphorically linked to an essential animality: "The Stock Exchange will be pulled down, the horse plough will give way to the tractor . . . the Eton and Harrow match will be forgotten, but England will still be England, an everlasting animal stretching into the future and the past, and, like all living things, having the power to change out of recognition and yet remain the same."[174] The unspoken message of *Animal Farm* is that England will weather the storms of the postwar world only if the English people do not cease believing in England and Englishness as a living, enduring creature. In terms of allegorical dualism of Orwell's beast fable, the pigs are positioned at the land's end of the familiar reality being changed "out of recognition," while the humbler animals, never giving up hope (109), collectively embody a national determination to "remain the same." If the extreme political humanization of the pigs fixes the reader's attention on the transformative power of futuristic, city-generated ideologies, the very limited and apparently temporary political humanization of the other farm creatures—a humanness usually balanced by reminders of animality (such as the tendency to experience reality as a permanent present, the predominance of biological needs, freedom as the ability to act in accordance with species-specific behavioral patterns)—awakens a reader's romantic nostalgia for a happier rural past.[175]

The setting of *Animal Farm* makes it a special type of beast fable. A farm provides that kind of boundaried space necessary both to control the referential direction of allegorical meaning and to establish a pastoral mood of ordered naturalness. Although against the grain of most serious fiction of the modernist period, which favored as its settings either the contemporary metropolis or exotic locales on the remote edges of Western civilization, the rustic Edwardian setting of Orwell's beast fable is suited to the generation of various meanings. If it is the cold comfort farm of the modern totalitarian state (primarily the Soviet Union peasantry being ruthlessly collectivized, but also a vision of the Nazi ideal of a de-urbanized Germany restored to its sturdy, obedient Aryan peasantry), it is also the type of workaday setting suitable for reminding the reader with socialist leanings (and who might vote Labor) that the heady wine of melioristic socialism must be mixed with water drawn from the well—not Wells—of hard work and austerity.

During the late thirties and early forties several other factors were contributing to the potential thematic and tonal resonance of the literary farm. In the Soviet Union the farmer and his land were still being exploited by the city: collectivized farms were forced to sell products to the state at a low fixed price, and the peasants' finest products were destined either for export to pay for industrial equipment or for consumption by the industrial worker. And in England a resurgent cultural conservatism was bringing with it an elegiac awareness of the disappearing rural, Victorian England. Balancing these negative situations were two positive ones that may have had some influence on Orwell's choice of a farm setting. To some extent *Animal Farm* celebrates the spirit of an alternative, non-Marxist but also anti-industrial and anticapitalist Russian communist movement that might have once served (and in the uncertain 1940s might still serve) as a counterweight to Stalinist centralization. This was the Narodniki movement, a federation of peasant-organized communes.[176] Also, as Orwell noted in a BBC broadcast, the British wartime land allotment program was turning the English urbanite back to the soil—with thousands of men having abandoned pub and dart game for the vegetable garden.[177] Surely Orwell then felt that his reading public would be especially receptive to the dual meaning of his rustic fable—the bad news of the political allegory tempered by the good news of the pastoral vision.

Moreover, the name Manor Farm suggests the broad historical significance of the fable's Edwardian setting. Orwell's "Manor" alludes not simply to England's agricultural life but also to the analysis of England's history from the early sixteenth century to the twentieth in Hilaire Belloc's *The Servile State*—the "astonishing accuracy" of which deeply impressed Orwell.[178] *Animal Farm* opens trailing clouds of Belloc's historical survey from the Tudor dispossession of church lands and their distribution among a minority of wealthy pro-Tudor landholders—an event Belloc viewed as a fateful derailing of an earlier, socially democratizing process in which small farmers had been gradually buying property from large estates. Belloc saw this gradual development as having been blocked by the sudden rise of the Tudor-enriched great manorial houses; and with wealth thus concentrated in the hands of a few, the later industrial revolution only solidified the division of society into its modern form as the "servile state"—in which a minority, owning the means of production, is able to force a hapless, unpropertied majority to work under conditions imposed by the few (58–59, 61, 65).

The prerevolutionary Manor Farm may be viewed as the final decadent stage of a long period of Manorial dominance. The juxtaposition of Farmer Jones's slumbering with the literal and figurative reveille to which the animals vigorously respond can be taken as the allegorical vision of an English Narodniki movement—a vision of the common man's long-interrupted egalitarian history breaking through the soil and continuing to grow if not blighted by the neo-manorialism of an essentially reactionary and antidemocratic Marxist socialism (the latter possibility suggested by Napoleon's cheerful reinstitution of the name Manor Farm [117]).

Animal Farm exhibits a start-stop-start pattern corresponding to such a vision of history. The animal singing that interrupts the slumber of Farmer Jones (whose own economic, if not personal, life seems to have been rudely jolted by a lawsuit) is in turn temporarily silenced by his shotgun; the course of animal democratization is sidetracked by the pigs' self-centered behavior and by external dangers that encourage a Stalinization of the farm; the dream of technological modernization is set back by the destruction of the windmill; Boxer's anticipation of a well-earned retirement is to be cruelly canceled out by the knacker's knife; and even a card game cannot be played out to

e—like the Orwell of *Homage to Catalonia*, for whom a mes-
ing pool in the garden of a Spanish hospital turns into the "cess-
of factional violence from which his imagination seems unable
ape (149, 189)—tries to save herself from a political role by
to town (*Animal Farm*, 39–40). The magnetic power of political
ry is underscored by the futility of her escape, since in town she
hes the allegorical representation of a recognizable historical
—the White Russian community pleasantly exiled in Paris after
volution. With one hoof in the world of the sarcastic Eeyore, the
y of A. A. Milne's *Pooh* stories, Ben tries to preserve a silence
vould confirm his extraliterary animality, but this silence gives
-more often than Orwell cares to admit—to utterances that place
mong contemporary intellectuals unavoidably involved in poli-
uch as Silone, Koestler, and Orwell himself.[184] Other animals are
successfully resistant to the pull of political allegorization. Al-
absent from the Bible's symbolic menagerie and, as Kipling has
s, the one animal that by nature walks alone, Orwell's nameless
ongs, along with the rats and the birds, to the anonymous realm
latory animality that needs neither man nor his political myths.
uring the course of the narrative even a structure, the Red Lion
dergoes a renovation for political use. As the scene of the drink-
t starts Farmer Jones on the path toward personal ruin, Or-
Red Lion merges with the Red Lion inn of Kenneth Grahame's
ind in the Willows, where the rash Mr. Toad initiates his own
t into humiliation and terror by stealing a motor car. In a real
—a Marxist study of English Chartism Orwell reviewed in No-
1937—it was in taverns that frustrated workers began orga-
hemselves for collective action against exploitation.[185] And if
ertainties of leftist revolutionary activism is suggested by a pos-
ference to another Red Lion inn, the one in Holborn, London,
he disinterred bodies of Oliver Cromwell and other regicides
posed before being desecrated, the persistence of left-wing ac-
suggested by the fact that even in the 1930s London's Red
quare (and presumably the public house with the same name)
athering place of leftist poets.[186]

the end without the violent disruption of exposed cheating. But balancing the stops are the starts and continuations—the worker animals'
fashioning of a community at least a little better than Jones's farm and
their enduring longing for a more just society.

Another kind of interruption, one relevant to the style of *Animal
Farm*, is that of the private dream language which, on awakening and
growing up, we are all forced to exchange for the "language of others."[179] The new language forcing itself on the awareness of the writer
indebted to the language of the Victorians and modernists was that of
the 1930s sociopolitical rhetoric—authoritatively abstract in its ability
to martial facts and figures into grand generalizations (usually Marxist),[180] activist and instrumental in persuading listener and reader to
support a partisan cause, and sometimes crudely authoritarian in en-
gaging in a verbal bullying that would roughly elbow aside the language of sober logic.

If Old Major's talk is concretely descriptive in cataloging the specific abuses and miseries suffered by Jones's animals, it is also manip-
ulative in implanting in the minds of his uncritical listeners absolutist
generalizations that will, for better or worse, predispose them to collective violence—that man is the only threat to animals and that men
and beasts have no interests in common (*Animal Farm*, 8–9). In *Mein
Kampf* Hitler claims that a passionate speaker could change history,
and so compelling are Old Major's sweeping generalizations that no
one present thinks to ask how the boar's admittedly lengthy periods
of isolation square with his claim of an unsurpassed knowledge of life
(6). Perhaps even more damaging to public life than the falsehoods
routinely presented as solemn truth by ideologues and propagandists,
an abuse of language Orwell was tireless in exposing, was the perver-
sion of language into a vehicle of aggressiveness and hatred. A month
after the completion of *Animal Farm*, Orwell expressed shock at the
willingness of English-speaking leftists to disfigure their political vocabulary with alien terms of abuse (mainly from the Russian) usually
meaningless in the context of British social experience: "Just talk
about hydra-headed jackboots riding roughshod over blood-stained

hyenas, and you are all right."[181] Implicit to the jargon term "coccidio-sis" (a type of animal disease caused by parasites) used to cover up the murder of rebellious hens by Napoleon's killer dogs (65) is the power that politics can wield over language and apolitical nature: with "par-asite" being a stock term of foreign extremist invective—the ousted human exploiters are called "parasitical" (24)—the attribution of the hens' deaths to coccidiosis metaphorically exalts both a brutal murder and a tragic commonplace of barnyard life into a privileged moment in the struggle of class against class.

However, in the language of beast fable, animal story, and fairy tale Orwell found a primal simplicity resistant to the pull of sociopolit-ical abstraction and partisan invective. In *Animal Farm* the straight-forward syntax and steady, low-keyed tone of the narrative even in descriptions of grievous events convey both the narrator's "sympa-thetic detachment" and the "doggedness" of the animals' will to endure.[182]

Two impulses at work in *Animal Farm* are the politically allegor-ical, the exposure of the totalitarian nature of a specifically Stalinist and generally Bonapartist socialism and the pastoral—the latter term including a number of literary conventions and themes resonant enough to expand the reader's focus from the narrowly political and topical to the broadly archetypal. It should be noted that political al-legorization is a development that takes place somewhere during the course of the narrative as a whole and never entirely absorbs the story. The opening scene of the tipsy Jones could just as well introduce a comically realistic novel of farm life, and even the assembly of animals of different species able to understand another animal's utterances ac-cords with the conventions of the animal story. Only when Old Major veers away from the simple description of his dream, an experience basic enough to be immediately understood by fowl and mammal alike, to a polemical rhetoric dealing with the alienation of animals from human beings that events invite an allegorical interpretation. And even then the futuristic vision that grips the animals' imagination is of an essentially nonallegorical condition—of a world that, being

without human beings, could not be allegorical in of the term. Conditioned by Old Major's politic (including this writer) sometimes mistakenly reg confrontation of man and animal—the hunger-dri ing into the feed shed and their instinctively self-p the men's attack—as a political and therefore p event. However, it is not until around the time c encounter that the behavior of the animals exhit humanly political—the creation of a command str planning, the development of both an organiza and an inspiriting ethos precisely formulated ir ideology.

Years earlier Orwell noted in regard to the I on tramps in public dormitories that in London " bed" were mutually exclusive.[183] In *Animal Far* doned bed and the house around it are at firs symbol of human oppression, and it is only wit curious animals first enter it. In crossing the thi fore human structure, an animal exposes itself tc of human meanings and thus becomes allegori: way that the humanizing operation performed the beasts in his laboratory turn them into : types corresponding to the respectable middle-c image of the urban lower classes. It is more tha first in-house animal, Moses the raven, had b an allegorical role several millenia earlier in tl the same is true of the houseward- and bedw obsession with the trappings of human politic: in the Gospel stories of evil spirits passing fror of swine (Matt. 8:28, Mark 5:13, Luke 8:26–

Some of the animals seem conscious of tl tween political allegory and their apolitical a resist being drawn into the allegory. Perhaps into which she gazes a future political cess

At the end of *Animal Farm* there appears an unmistakable separation between the politically allegorized animals and those that are returning home to their primal animality. Enclosed in the farm house of their politicized identities, the pigs are oblivious of their former comrades outside, and the latter—the humble worker animals in the open air—are as far removed from events inside the human structure as is Heathcliff from the human life in the residences in *Wuthering Heights.*

THE CHILD'S VISION OF REALITY

A trait of Dickens that greatly impressed Orwell was the former's ability to re-create a child's view of reality, and in noting this skill in "Charles Dickens" Orwell suggests the Victorian's ability to awaken within the adult reader a child's responsiveness to life. The morally educative power of this literary skill is not lost on the anxious post-Victorian: "If you hate violence and don't believe in politics, the only major remedy is education. Perhaps society is past praying for, but there is always hope for the individual human being, if you can catch him young."[187] The innocent at whom a morally responsible literature is to be directed is not simply the young in years but also the English common people, still by and large insulated from the political rancorousness of the Continent. However, although the "tolerance and decency" of the people "are deeply rooted," such qualities can wither away if not "kept alive partly by conscious effort," Orwell claims in the essay written to accompany the first edition of *Animal Farm*, "The Freedom of the Press," and he insists that the core of the English national psyche, its "instinct," must be kept protected from the atmosphere of violence and hatred generated as much by antifascists as by fascists.[188]

One problem facing the twentieth-century moralist is the grotesqueness of the realities which his imagination is attempting to control for literary purposes. The world of the modern allegorist is "full . . . of monstrous . . . forces."[189] The psychiatrist's explanation in

Wells's *The Croquet Player* regarding Dr. Finchatton's supposedly fabricated stories of village violence—that the doctor resorted to the "fairy tale" to control his anxiety at certain "monstrous and frightful" forebodings about to overwhelm him—suggests the usefulness of an impure beast fable in *Animal Farm,* with room for nonallegorized animal and human characters. If satire exposes and attacks, and if the fable conveys an intellectually coherent message, the emotionally charged animal story can sharpen a reader's affective response to the melodramatic excesses of the age while bringing into play his capacity for compassionate understanding. An example of the monstrous reality of contemporary political life is appropriate to the farmyard setting of *Animal Farm:* the gander that knows a dire punishment awaits it for allowing weeds to sprout in the wheat field (81) is the counterpart of the real Soviet agricultural officials summarily executed in March 1933 for a similar offence.[190]

The belief that insights into the darker areas of the human psyche can be gained from stories of animal mistreatment underlies Orwell's defence of the "maniacal logic" in Edgar Allan Poe's fiction. Regarding "The Black Cat" Orwell states that from the account of the drunkard's cutting out of the cat's eye the reader can tell why it was done and even becomes aware of his own capacity for a similar cruelty.[191] The presence in *Animal Farm* of the most Poesque of animals—the raven (first Jones's pet and then Napoleon's)—suggests an exploration into the emotional labyrinth leading to the "maniacal logic" of a ruler's cruelty.

That Orwell wanted *Animal Farm* to be part of a great tradition of modern literature extending beyond the tight scope of topical satire is hinted at by the image to which, in the preface to the Ukrainian edition of *Animal Farm,* he traced the later idea of a politicized beast fable—that of an English farm boy whipping a cart horse down a country road.[192] This image also derives from the works of two famous modernists in Orwell's library—Raskolnikov's terrible dream of a childhood scene in which drunken revellers beat a cart horse to death (in Dostoyevski's *Crime and Punishment,* 1886) and Stevie Verloc's anguished sight of a hackney horse being whipped (in Conrad's *The Secret Agent,* 1907). As satirical allegory *Animal Farm* taps the adult reader's springs of outrage and censure at the political evils behind the rustic fiction. As animal story, the work measures the reader's compassionate responsiveness to the sufferings of vulnerable beasts. Balancing the adult reader's condemnation of events and conditions revealed by the satirical allegory is the child's spontaneous and unconditional sympathy for the mistreated animal.

Although Orwell's Napoleon is routinely viewed as the object of satire because of his villainy, from the child's perspective—and from the perspective of a story favored by young Eric Blair, Beatrix Potter's *The Tale of Pigling Bland*[193]—Napoleon can be granted a degree of sympathy as a creature that circumstances have pushed out of the pastoral world of the youthful imagination into the fallen world of adult political history. Forced by Aunt Pettitoes' poverty onto the road to a nearby market town, Pigling Bland must not cross the county line—a point of no return. Napoleon's county line is the assumption of revolutionary leadership, which makes him—like the regicides of history—a marked pig for life. Pigling Bland's uncertain journey toward the market town and Napoleon's long march down the trail of revolutionary violence are equally perilous. The pathos implicit in Aunt Pettitoes' urging of Pigling always to walk upright might extend to Napoleon's bipedalism—a protective maneuver in a world full of menacing human beings. If Napoleon is allegorically the totalitarian ruler sinking ever deeper into a cesspool of political evil, he is also Potter's vulnerable hero who, having taken a "wrong turn—several wrong turns," is now "quite lost." The comparison even suggests something like an existential courage in Orwell's pig. Potter's tale is an escapist fantasy: finally Pigling and his sweetheart, Pig-wig, dance their way off the last page—"over the hills and far away"—into some metanarrative porcine idyll. Drunkenly running around the farmyard, Napoleon discovers himself caught in a closed world, the only far away hills offering a refuge being the superearthly "Sugarcandy Mountain" glibly promised by the unreliable Moses (90, 97). There really is no escape, and as both the farm's political leader and its only boar (94), Napoleon is trapped between treacherous humanity and, on the other side, the many piglings who—like the merciless rival determined to replace the old king in Frazer's *Golden Bough*—may eventually present a challenge to their sire's rule.

ANIMAL FARM AS PARABLE

"When we were droning away in school on a fine morning, it was paradise to hear all around the crowing of cocks and clucking of hens, mooing of cows and cawing of rooks. . . . But there was also . . . the painful screeching of some unfortunate pig aware of his doom."[194] Edmund Blunden's memory of his rural childhood calls attention to two antithetical realities of *Animal Farm*—pastoral as paradise and farm as place of terror-filled awareness. To combine these opposites into a significant vision of reality, one with a moral as well as political dimension, Orwell needed a form that could evoke a thoughtful, meditative response to the events of the narrative—the parable. To more fully appreciate the parabolic nature of *Animal Farm*—in which homely, commonplace events and situations allegorically suggest basic moral or spiritual truths—it will be useful to note the twentieth-century tendency to merge secular ideology with religious longing. In *Mein Kampf* Hitler, indifferent to most aspects of organized religion, waxed enthusiastic at the worldly uses of "religious fanaticism", and during the thirties and forties writers as ideologically different in their attitudes to Soviet communism as Borkenau and Laski detected a religious craving implicit in Marxist revolutionary activity and in Stalin's public image.[195] In "Freedom of the Press" Orwell points to the tendency of British intellectuals to regard as "blasphemy" any doubts about "sacrosanct" Stalin and to the intelligentsia's "worship of Russian militarism."[196]

The "fear and despair" of Orwell's animals at the destruction of their windmill and then their rage for revenge in *Animal Farm* (86) springs from religious feelings. The origin of the disappeared windmill is Eugene Lyons's account of the overnight blasting away (on 30 July 1929) of the Shrine of the Iberian Virgin—the "most famous and holiest shrine in all of Russia"—and the crowd of grieving faithful around the large hole just off Moscow's Red Square.[197] In Orwell this becomes the "big hole" left by the disappearance of the belief in immortality.[198] Basically agreeing with Borkenau's statement in *The Totalitarian Enemy* that some replacement for formal Christianity is needed to counter the religious fervor of totalitarian ideologies (142) and possibly inspired by John Macmurray's *A Clue to History* (1938), which describes Hebrew religion as this-worldly and not dependent on a belief in immortality and otherworldly rewards and punishments,[199] Orwell claimed soon after the completion of *Animal Farm* that real social progress must include the reaffirmation of an unbending morality unsupported by otherworldly sanctions.[200] Thinking backwards from an early 1946 article expressing Orwell's sympathy with the view that Christian virtues "flourish in small communities, where life is simple," rather than in a "highly complex, luxurious society,"[201] a reader may regard *Animal Farm* as a mixed parable—religious, humanistic, socialist—warning against those extravagant expectations of materialistic abundance that, planted in the minds of the common people, would render the soil of restraint and moderation useless for the cultivation of a humane morality.

From first to last in Orwell's writings—from the contrast between the patient Dr. Veriswami and the grasping U Po Kyin in *Burmese Days* to the difference between the rebellious Winston Smith and the docile proles in *Nineteen Eighty-Four*—two ways of experiencing reality are juxtaposed. One, the way of the West, is activist—the conscious effort by individuals or groups, driven by desire, to control and possess reality. The other way, ordinarily associated with the East, involves a passive acceptance of life and, if need be, an endurance of suffering. If, as indicated earlier in this study, Orwell's trips back to England can be regarded as homecomings, it may be just as true to regard Orwell's joining of the BBC India section in the early forties as a symbolic return to his original home. In talking to India Orwell may have been talking to the India in himself: he may have been accepting into consciousness a vision of life structured on polarities—Western attachment and Eastern detachment.

The angry command uttered seven times in a few minutes by Elizabeth Lackersteen to gain her freedom from Flory's grip as he tries to force her forgiveness, sympathy, and acceptance—"let me go!" (*Burmese Days*, 275–77)—is also a warning against desire. In *Gulliver's Travels* the "roar" of pain that Gulliver emits as a Houyhnhnm squeezes his hand becomes in *Animal Farm* the explicit charge that the "hand" is the distinguishing mark of human evildoing (29). Symbolic of the hand's responsibility for the alienation of propertyless animal from property-obsessed man is the repeated association of human callousness with the farm's five-barred gate that is shut against him and through which he constantly attempts to pass (17, 20, 85, 103). Symbolic of the pigs' absorption into the human condition of acquisitiveness is another kind of hand—the cheating hand of cards during the pigs and men's poker game (118).

Several millenia before *Animal Farm* the Buddha anticipated the theme of subdued desire versus foolish longing in his lesson to a young ox dissatisfied with his "grass and straw" while pigs grew fat on rice: being fattened for a wedding feast, the pig gets the "food of death," whereas the ox's coarse food "is a pledge that" his life "will not be cut short."[202] In Orwell's works eating is usually furtive and guilty because fleshiness betokens some form of desire—thus the extremes of ambition, lust, or power-hunger in such thick-bodied characters as U Po Kyin, Warburton, Flaxman (an adulterous traveling salesman in *Keep the Aspidistra Flying*), O'Brien, and, of course, the porcine Napoleon. Even though a number of Orwellian protagonists are slightly built (Flory, Dorothy Hare, Gordon Comstock, Winston Smith), their careers at times raise the suspicion that inside the thin person is a fat one trying to get out—to snowball.

This duality is grotesquely exaggerated in the career of Orwell's Napoleon. On the one hand a gourmandizing emblem of political power-hunger, on the other hand Napoleon is the victim-to-be of the Buddha's parable—food for human stomachs. "Bacon for breakfast is an English institution almost as old as parliamentary government," groans a bacon-weary Reverend Hare, and the "pig's head ready stewed" Dorothy is happy to receive from a charitable family of hop pickers (*A Clergyman's Daughter*, 21, 133) turns up again in George Bowling's adult recollection of his childhood meals (*Coming Up for Air*, 57). In *Animal Farm* the victorious beasts' solemn burial of Jones's hams does not, however, expunge the pigs' subliminal knowledge of what awaits them should the revolution fail. In fact, nothing can extricate the born victim from his bind: the very act consciously intended to insure and signify the pigs' control over the revolution—their claim on the tastiest and the richest food—is an unwitting submission to their alimentary destiny. Foreshadowed in *Down and Out in Paris and London* by the communist who once persisted in guzzling his employer's milk despite the serious health hazard involved (102–3), the weight gain supposed to enhance Napoleon's look of awesome power is also a fattening for the slaughter (95, 106). As mentioned in chapter 6, the rigors of hunting help Flory sweat out a mounting nihilism, and in *Assignment in Utopia* Lyons describes two ex-members of a brutal Soviet paramilitary organization whose feverish consumption of vodka seems motivated by a need to blunt their horror of past atrocities conjured up by drink (470–73). But neither whiskey nor a run around the yard can quell Napoleon's desperation: boozing simply increases the weight of the ham-to-be, and nothing can be sweated out of a pig—an animal without sweat glands. The pig being an important wartime food source—indeed government-regulated "pig clubs" sprang up in towns and cities to meet a growing demand for pig flesh[203]—Orwell's original readers could have predicted Napoleon's future as either food or the producer of food as procreative counterpart of the modern slaves of Belloc's *The Servile State*. The truth suggested by the myopic Clover's view of Napoleon indistinguishable from man is that a real pig can become human in only one way—by being devoured.

The Eastern cycle of birth and rebirth into earthly existence to which an individual remains bound unless he is able at some point to detach himself through virtuous behavior and the subduing of intemperate craving;[204] the Shakespearian "massy wheel" of state that, collapsing, brings ruin on ruler and subjects alike *(Hamlet)*, or the "wheel of fire" that torments even the great of the earth *(King Lear)*; the "incessant wheels" of "blind" determinism that destroy Wells's scientist as well as his victims *(The Island of Doctor Moreau)*—from any of these sources Orwell might have derived the motif of circularity linked to too close an involvement with the world. In *Burmese Days* the disruptive intrusiveness.of Western acquisitive materialism into the East is connoted by the strident sound given off by the white colonials' gramophone discs (209)—an image used later in the thirties to characterize the thousands of leftist propagandists mindlessly repeating the party line,[205] and in *A Clergyman's Daughter* Dorothy Hare's passage from a semi-idyllic existence as amnesiac and field worker back and to the dead-alive condition of money-consciousness is marked by her participation in a ring dance around a bonfire (155).

In *Animal Farm* cyclic imagery is associated with the moral dangers of an obsessive revolutionary activism. The Napoleon racing drunkenly around the farmyard (90) is a creature imprisoned in his own egocentric craving for power. That an atmosphere of senseless violence may be spreading to the humbler animals' imaginations—perhaps even to their actual behavior—is suggested by the sheep's confession of having chased a sickly old ram around a bonfire until he died (71). If the windmill is tightly bound up with Snowball's tempting vision of an electrified and effortless paradise, the turning blades signify history's inconstancy, with the bend sinister of primitive impulse turning the revolutionary propagandist's progressive futuristic myth of unidirectional movement into at best a flattened upward spiral.

The general movement of *Animal Farm* is toward a division of the animal community into those creatures mired in the pitch of worldliness—the pigs (as well as their human counterparts) gripped by a craving at all costs to gain the upper hand by displaying a winning one—and those beasts who maintain a balance between a proud attachment to their unique social experiment and a basically passive, quietist acceptance of their workaday existence as toilers working their collective half acre (109–10). The widening gap in the narrative between the politically allegorized pigs and the producing beasts drawing back into their ancient identities of domesticated animality becomes a parabolic field. From the honeyed and then rancorous utterances of the mutually suspicious groups of schemers inside the farmhouse and the puzzled silence of the unnoticed spectators in the farmyard arises the implicit lesson that to save its collective soul England (and by extension the democratic West) must preserve the pastoral qualities of acceptance and endurance as a check on the restless craving of modern revolutionary man for ever more extreme—and therefore ultimately self-subverting—political goals.

NOTES

1. Richard Mayne, review of *George Orwell: A Personal Memoir* (T. R. Fyvel), *Times Literary Supplement* (London), 26 November 1982, 1292.

2. Preface to the Ukrainian edition of *Animal Farm*, in *The Collected Essays, Journalism and Letters of George Orwell*, ed. Sonia Orwell and Ian Angus (New York: Harcourt, Brace & World, 1968), 3:404–5. In further notes this volume will be cited as *Collected Essays*.

3. "As I Please," 24 December 1943; in *Collected Essays*, 3:64.

4. Cyril Connolly, review of *Animal Farm*, September 1945, in *George Orwell: The Critical Heritage*, ed. Jeffrey Meyers (London: Routledge & Kegan Paul, 1975), 201.

5. Alex Zwerdling, *Orwell and the Left* (New Haven, Conn.: Yale University Press, 1974), 90.

6. Jeffrey Meyers, *A Reader's Guide to George Orwell* (London: Thames & Hudson, 1975), 74, 78; J. R. Hammond, *A George Orwell Companion* (London: Macmillan, 1982), 161–62; Lutz Büthe, *Auf den Spuren George Orwells: eine soziale Biographie* (Hamburg: Junius Verlag, 1984), 284.

7. Roberta Kalechofsky, *George Orwell* (New York: Frederick Ungar, 1973), 100; Edward M. Thomas, *Orwell* (New York: Barnes & Noble, 1967), 71.

8. Henry Judd, "*Animal Farm*—A Good Fable with a Misdirected Moral," *Labor Action*, 30 September 1946, 6.

9. John Atkins, *George Orwell: A Literary and Biographical Study* (New York: Frederick Ungar, 1954), 222.

10. Stephen J. Ingle, "The Politics of George Orwell: A Reappraisal," *Queen's Quarterly* 80, no. 1 (1973):30.

11. Zwerdling, *Orwell and the Left*, 89–90.

12. *Collected Essays*, 1:413.

13. Paul Gray, "That Year Is Almost Here," *Time,* 28 November 1983, 47.

14. See, for example, Norman Podhoretz, "If Orwell Were Alive Today," *Harper's,* January 1983, 30–37.

15. Christopher Norris, ed., *Inside the Myth; Orwell: Views from the Left* (London: Lawrence & Wishart, 1984).

16. W. J. Turner, "How It Happened," *Spectator,* 17 August 1945, 156.

17. Anthony Edward Dyson, "Orwell: Irony as Prophecy," in *The Crazy Fabric: Essays on Irony* (New York: St. Martin's Press, 1965), 206.

18. Christopher Small, *The Road to Miniluv: George Orwell, the State and God* (London: Victor Gollancz, 1975), 106.

19. Christopher Hollis, *A Study of George Orwell* (Chicago: Henry Regnery, 1956), 150–51.

20. Richard J. Voorhees, *The Paradox of George Orwell* (West Lafayette, Ind.: Purdue University, 1961), 23.

21. Hammond, *George Orwell Companion,* 162.

22. Sean O'Casey, *Sunset and Evening Star* (New York: Macmillan, 1954), 140.

23. "The Frontiers of Art and Propaganda," 30 April 1941, in *Collected Essays,* 2:126; review of *Burnt Norton, East Coker,* and *The Dry Salvages* (T. S. Eliot), October-November 1942, in *Collected Essays,* 2:239–40.

24. *Collected Essays,* 1:6, 7.

25. For example, Ellen Douglas Leyburn, *Satiric Allegory: Mirror of Man* (New Haven, Conn.: Yale University Press, 1956), 68–70; Gilbert Highet, *The Anatomy of Satire* (Princeton, N.J.: Princeton University Press, 1962), 185–86; Angus Fletcher, *Allegory: The Theory of a Symbolic Mode* (Ithaca, N.Y.: Cornell University Press, 1964), 158; Matthew Hodgart, *Satire* (New York: World University Library, 1969), 24, 176; Margaret Blount, *Animal Land: The Creatures of Children's Fiction* (London: Hutchinson, 1974), 66; H. J. Blackham, *The Fable as Literature* (London: Athlone Press, 1985), 135–37.

26. Northrop Frye, review of *Animal Farm,* December 1946, in Meyers, *Orwell: The Critical Heritage,* 207–8.

27. G. S. Fraser, *The Modern Writer and His World* (London: Derek Verschoyle, 1953), 131.

28. Richard Rees, *George Orwell: Fugitive from the Camp of Victory* (London: Secker & Warburg, 1961), 92.

29. Rama Rani Lall, *Satiric Fable: A Critical Study of the Animal Tales of Chaucer, Spenser, Dryden, and Orwell* (New Delhi: New Statesman, 1979), 125.

30. Isaac Rosenfeld, review of *Animal Farm,* 7 September 1946, in

Notes

Meyers, *Orwell: The Critical Heritage*, 203; Alan Dutscher, "Orwell and the Crisis of Responsibility," *Contemporary Issues* 8 (1956):311; John A. Morris, *Writers and Politics in Modern Britain* (London: Hodder & Stoughton, 1977), 83; Stephen Sedley, "An Immodest Proposal: *Animal Farm*," in Norris, *Inside the Myth*, 156.

31. Laurence Brander, introduction to *"Animal Farm": A Fairy Story* (London: Longmans, Green, 1960), xviii.

32. Jenni Calder, *Chronicles of Conscience: A Study of George Orwell and Arthur Koestler* (London: Secker & Warburg, 1968), 225; Robert A. Lee, *Orwell's Fiction* (Notre Dame, Ind.: University of Notre Dame Press, 1969), 108.

33. Luke Spencer, "*Animal Farm* and *Nineteen Eighty-Four*," in *George Orwell*, ed. J. A. Jowitt and R. K. S. Taylor, Bradford Occasional Papers, no. 3 (October 1981), 70.

34. Richard I. Smyer, *Primal Dream and Primal Crime: Orwell's Development as a Psychological Novelist* (Columbia: University of Missouri Press, 1979), 107; David Morgan Zehr, "Orwell and the Proles: Revolutionary or Middle-Class Voyeur?," *Centennial Review* 27 (Winter 1983):35.

35. Lynette Hunter, *George Orwell: The Search for a Voice* (Stony Stratford, Milton Keynes, England: Open University Press, 1984), 188.

36. Alan Sandison, *The Last Man in Europe: An Essay on George Orwell* (London: Macmillan, 1974), 154.

37. For a discussion of this trend, see Gillian Workman, "Orwell Criticism," *Ariel: A Review of International English Literature* 3, no. 1 (1972):62–73.

38. Richard Cook, "Rudyard Kipling and George Orwell," *Modern Fiction Studies* 7 (Summer 1961):125–35; Myrddin Jones, "Orwell, Wells and the Animal Fable," *English* 33 (Summer 1984):127–36; Timothy Cook, "Upton Sinclair's *The Jungle* and George Orwell's *Animal Farm:* A Relationship Explored," *Modern Fiction Studies* 30 (Winter 1984):696–703.

39. Frank W. Wadsworth, "Orwell as a Novelist: Orwell's Later Work," *University of Kansas City Review* 22 (June 1956):285; Morris, *Writers and Politics*, 83.

40. W. G. Müller, "Formen des Alogischen in George Orwells *Animal Farm*," *Literatur in Wissenschaft und Unterricht* 12, no. 1 (1979):22–36.

41. Angela Praesent, *George Orwell: Krise der Selbstverständlichkeit* (Heidelberg: Carl Winter, 1978), 35, 41.

42. Hunter, *George Orwell*, 162–90.

43. Daphne Patai, *The Orwell Mystique: A Study in Male Ideology* (Amherst: University of Massachusetts Press, 1984), 201–18.

44. Bernard Crick, *George Orwell: A Life* (London: Secker & Warburg, 1980), 302–25.

45. Michael Shelden, ed., *Ten "Animal Farm" Letters to His Agent, Leonard Moore* (Bloomington, Ind.: Fredric Brewer, 1984).

46. W. J. West, ed., *Orwell: The War Broadcasts* (London: Duckworth/BBC, 1985); West, ed., *Orwell: The War Commentaries* (London: Duckworth/BBC, 1985).

47. Orwell to T. S. Elliot, 28 June 1944; Orwell to Leonard Moore, 18 July 1944, in *Collected Essays*, 3:176, 186–87.

48. "A Good Word for the Vicar of Bray," 26 April 1946, in *Collected Essays*, 4:151.

49. *Collected Essays*, 1:4, 7.

50. Ibid., 1:424–25.

51. William Empson, *Some Versions of Pastoral* (London: Chatto & Windus, 1968), 22.

52. Crick, *George Orwell*, 194.

53. Ibid., 11, 194.

54. Orwell to Jack Common, 5 July 1938, in *Collected Essays*, 1:338–39.

55. Ibid., 1:355.

56. "As I Please," 5 May 1944, in *Collected Essays*, 3:144–45.

57. Paul Potts, *Dante Called You Beatrice* (London: Eyre & Spottiswoode, 1960), 75.

58. David L. Kubal, *Outside the Whale: George Orwell's Art and Politics* (Notre Dame, Ind.: University of Notre Dame Press, 1972), 124.

59. Sandison, *Last Man in Europe*, 9.

60. Empson, *Some Versions of Pastoral*, 187.

61. *Collected Essays*, 1:368–70.

62. Henry Popkin, "Orwell the Edwardian," *Kenyon Review* 16, no. 1 (1954):139.

63. Bernard Bergonzi, *The Situation of the Novel*, 2d ed. (London: Macmillan, 1979), 150.

64. T. R. Fyvel, *George Orwell: A Personal Memoir* (London: Hutchinson, 1983), 196.

65. *Collected Essays*, 2:186.

66. John Wain, "George Orwell (II)," in *Essays on Literature and Ideas* (London: Macmillan, 1963), 199.

67. *Collected Essays*, 1:388.

68. "Countryman's World," review of *The Way of a Countryman* (Sir William Beach Thomas), *Manchester Evening News*, 23 March 1944, 2.

69. Anthony West, "George Orwell," in *Principles and Persuasions: The Literary Essays of Anthony West* (London: Eyre & Spottiswoode, 1958), 159.

Notes

70. *Manchester Evening News*, 29 March 1944.

71. Peter Stansky and William Abrahams, *The Unknown Orwell* (New York: Alfred A. Knopf, 1972).

72. *Collected Essays*, 2:164.

73. Literary notebook no. 3 (1949), in Orwell Archive, University College, London.

74. Calder, *Chronicles of Conscience*, 89–90; Laurence Brander, *George Orwell* (London: Longmans, Green, 1954), 98, 100; Hammond, *George Orwell Companion*, 101; Sandison, *Last Man in Europe*, 14.

75. *Collected Essays*, 1:6, 450–51.

76. Empson, *Some Versions of Pastoral*, 6.

77. Peter Keating, introduction to *Into Unknown England 1866–1913*, ed. Peter Keating (Manchester, England: Manchester University Press, 1976), 20.

78. George Woodcock, *The Crystal Spirit: A Study of George Orwell* (Boston: Little, Brown, 1966), 132.

79. *Collected Essays*, 1:67.

80. Sir James George Frazer, *The Golden Bough: A Study in Magic and Religion*, abridged ed. (New York: Macmillan, 1940), 400–1.

81. Ibid., 646–47.

82. Review of *The Rock Pool* (Cyril Connolly) and *Almayer's Folly* (Joseph Conrad), 23 July 1936, in *Collected Essays*, 1:226.

83. Beatrix Campbell, "Orwell—Paterfamilias or Big Brother?" in *Inside the Myth*, 133; Patai, *Orwell Mystique*, 107.

84. *Collected Essays*, 1:2.

85. "The Road to Wigan Pier Diary" (1936), in *Collected Essays*, 1:191, 196; *The Road to Wigan Pier*, 107.

86. *Collected Essays*, 3:2.

87. "Notes on the Way," 6 April 1940, in *Collected Essays*, 2:15.

88. Crick, *George Orwell*, 201.

89. Christopher Caudwell, *Illusion and Reality: A Study of the Sources of Poetry* (London: Lawrence & Wishart, 1947), 70, 163.

90. John Strachey, *The Coming Struggle for Power* (New York: Covici, Friede, 1933), 348.

91. J. D. Bernal, *The World, the Flesh and the Devil: An Enquiry into the Future of the Three Enemies of the Rational Soul*, 2d ed. (Bloomington: Indiana University Press, 1969), 12, 18–22.

92. "Boys' Weeklies," March 1940; abridged in *Collected Essays*, 1:475.

93. H. G. Wells, *A Modern Utopia* (New York: Charles Scribner's Sons, 1905), 100–2.

94. Leon Trotsky, *The Revolution Betrayed: What Is the Soviet Union and Where Is It Going?*, trans. Max Eastman (Garden City, N.Y.: Doubleday, Doran, 1937), 8; Bertrand Russell, *The Practice and Theory of Bolshevism* (1920; reprint, London: George Allen & Unwin, 1949), 35, n. 1.

95. Kalechofsky, *Orwell*, 105; Lee, *Orwell's Fiction*, 117–18.

96. "The Meaning of a Poem," 12 June 1941, in *Collected Essays*, 2:132–33.

97. "Wells, Hitler and the World State," August 1941, in *Collected Essays*, 2:142.

98. Francis Bacon, *The Moral and Historical Works*, ed. Joseph Devey (London: George Bell & Sons, 1894), 298.

99. H. G. Wells, *What Are We To Do with Our Lives?* (Garden City, N.Y.: Doubleday, Doran, 1931), 50.

100. Francis J. Sheed, *Communism and Man* (New York: Sheed & Ward, 1938), 70.

101. H. G. Wells, *The Shape of Things to Come: The Ultimate Revolution* (London: Hutchinson, 1935), 321.

102. Ibid., 271, 311–12, 326.

103. Strachey, *The Coming Struggle*, 141.

104. Bernal, *The World, the Flesh and the Devil*, 36–39.

105. H. G. Wells, *New Worlds for Old* (London: Archibald Constable, 1908), 22.

106. Wells, *A Modern Utopia*, 113–29.

107. Kenneth Clark, *Animals and Men: Their Relationship as Reflected in Western Art from Prehistory to the Present Day* (London: Thames & Hudson, 1977), 53.

108. Preface to the Ukrainian edition of *Animal Farm*, in *Collected Essays*, 3:405–6.

109. *Collected Essays*, 1:392.

110. Blount, *Animal Land*, 24.

111. Literary notebook no. 1 (1939/40–1946/47), Orwell Archive, University College, London.

112. "War-time Diary," 12 April 1940, in *Collected Essays*, 2:374.

113. *Collected Essays*, 1:238, 240.

114. Ibid., 1:239, 240.

115. Ibid., 1:241.

116. Kubal, *Outside the Whale*, 77.

117. Edwin Muir, "The Natural and the Political Man," in *Essays on Literature and Society* (London: Hogarth Press, 1965), 158. It is quite likely that Orwell read this important essay on its first publication, in 1942, in John

Notes

Lehmann's *New Writing and Daylight,* a serial publication with which Orwell was familiar.

118. Adolph Hitler, *Mein Kampf,* trans. Helmut Ripperger et al. (New York: Reynal & Hitchcock, 1939), 389.

119. Ibid., 605.

120. Ibid., 591.

121. Russell, *Practice and Theory of Bolshevism,* 98.

122. Harold J. Laski, *Communism* (New York: Henry Holt, 1927), 173.

123. John McGovern, *Terror in Spain: How the Communist International Has Destroyed Working Class Unity* (London: Independent Labor Party, 1938), 14.

124. August 1941, *Collected Essays,* 2:143.

125. H. G. Wells, *The Croquet Player* (New York: Viking Press, 1937), 64, 69.

126. John Sommerfield, *Volunteer in Spain* (London: Lawrence & Wishart, 1937), 103.

127. "Notes on the Way," 6 April 1940, in *Collected Essays,* 2:15.

128. Russell, *Practice and Theory of Bolshevism,* 19.

129. Philip Henderson, *The Novel Today: Studies in Contemporary Attitudes* (1936; reprint, London: Norwood Editions, 1978), 49.

130. "As I Please," 28 April 1944, in *Collected Essays,* 3:133.

131. Review of *Mein Kampf* (Adolph Hitler), 21 March 1940, in *Collected Essays,* 2:1.

132. Ignazio Silone, *The School for Dictators,* trans. Gwenda David and Eric Mosbacher (New York: Harper & Bros, 1938), 81.

133. B[oris] Souvarine, *Cauchemar en U.R.S.S.* (Paris: Revue de Paris, 1937), 41.

134. Stansky and Abrahams, *Unknown Orwell,* 115.

135. Silone, *The School for Dictators,* 93.

136. Radio adaptation of "The Fox," by Ignazio Silone, *War Broadcasts,* 139–48.

137. Bertrand Russell, *Power: A New Social Analysis* (New York: W. W. Norton, 1938), 19.

138. Souvarine, *Cauchemar,* 42.

139. Silone, *School for Dictators,* 81.

140. Edward Hulton, *The New Age* (London: G. Allen & Unwin, 1943), 75.

141. Orwell to Cyril Connolly, 1 December 1937 and 27 April 1938, in *Collected Essays,* 1:290, 329; Orwell to Stephen Spender [15] April 1938, in *Collected Essays,* 1:313.

142. *Collected Essays,* 2:303.

143. Review of *The Two Carlyles* (Osbert Burdett), March 1931, in *Collected Essays,* 1:36.

144. "Politics vs. Literature: An Examination of *Gulliver's Travels,*" September 1946, in *Collected Essays,* 4:220.

145. Orwell to Brenda Salkeld, [September] 1934, in *Collected Essays,* 1:140.

146. *Collected Essays,* 1:35.

147. "Jonathan Swift, an Imaginary Interview," in *War Broadcasts,* 113, 116.

148. 12 July 1940, *Collected Essays,* 2:30.

149. October 1944, *Collected Essays,* 3:216.

150. *War Broadcasts,* 98.

151. Ibid., 120, 170–71.

152. *Collected Essays,* 3:160, 163.

153. Ibid., 1:226.

154. "Fascism and Democracy," in *The Betrayal of the Left,* ed. Victor Gollancz (London: Gollancz, 1941), 215.

155. *Collected Essays,* 3:7–13, 30–31.

156. Hodgart, *Satire,* 30.

157. *Collected Essays,* 3:160.

158. Ibid., 4:221–23.

159. Ibid., 3:105.

160. Ibid., 3:158–59, 164.

161. Ibid., 1:119.

162. Ibid., 2:319.

163. Ibid., 3:237.

164. William Langland, prologue to *Piers the Plowman,* trans. Margaret Williams (New York: Random House, 1971), 17–19.

165. *Collected Essays,* 2:249–67.

166. John Gay, "The Gardener and the Hog," in *John Gay: Poetry and Prose,* vol. 2, *Fables,* ed. Vinton A. Dearing (Oxford: Clarendon Press, 1974), 367.

167a. This "Special issue report" is quoted in W. J. West's introduction to *War Commentaries,* 20–22.

167b. "The Freedom of the Press," *Times* [of London] *Literary Supplement,* 15 September 1972, 1039.

168. Gay Clifford, *The Transformations of Allegory* (London: Routledge & Kegan Paul, 1974), 47.

169. *Collected Essays,* 1:6.

Notes

170. Ibid., 1:450, 454.

171. Winwood Reade, *The Martyrdom of Man* (New York: E. P. Dutton, 1926), 453.

172. Arthur Koestler, "The Yogi and the Commissar," in *The Yogi and the Commissar and Other Essays* (New York: Macmillan, 1945), 5–6.

173. "The Intellectual Revolt (1)," *Manchester Evening News,* 24 January 1946, 2.

174. *Collected Essays,* 2:78.

175. Blount, *Animal Land,* 131:32.

176. Franz Borkenau, *World Communism: A History of the Communist International* (New York: W. W. Norton, 1939), 34–40. This was reviewed by Orwell on 22 September 1938 under the title "The Communist International."

177. "Money and Guns," 20 January 1942, in *War Broadcasts,* 73.

178. "Notes on the Way," 6 April 1940, in *Collected Essays,* 2:16.

179. Irving Massey, *The Gaping Pig: Literature and Metamorphosis* (Berkeley: University of California Press, 1976), 30.

180. For a discussion of Orwell's criticism of contemporary language use, see Charles Scruggs, "George Orwell and Jonathan Swift: A Literary Relationship," *South Atlantic Quarterly* 76 (Spring 1977):178–81.

181. "As I Please," 17 March 1944, in *Collected Essays,* 3:110–11.

182. Calder, *Chronicles of Conscience,* 225–26.

183. "Common Lodging Houses," 3 September 1932, in *Collected Essays,* 1:98.

184. For the political implications of Ben's reading ability, see Smyer, *Primal Dream and Primal Crime,* 107–9.

185. Neil Stewart, *The Fight for the Charter* (London: Chapman & Hall, 1937), 21, 106–7.

186. Stanley Weintraub, *The Last Great Cause: The Intellectuals and the Spanish Civil War* (New York: Weybright & Talley, 1968), 80.

187. *Collected Essays,* 1:423–24.

188. "The Freedom of the Press," *Times* [of London] *Literary Supplement,* 15 September 1972, 1038.

189. Rex Warner, "The Cult of Power," in *The Cult of Power* (London: John Lane, Bodley Head, 1946), 118.

190. Souvarine, *Cauchemar,* 35.

191. "Inside the Whale," 1940, in *Collected Essays,* 1:523.

192. *Collected Essays,* 4:406.

193. Jacintha Buddicom, *Eric and Us: A Remembrance of George Orwell* (London: Leslie Frewin, 1974), 39.

194. Edmund Blunden, "Country Childhood," in *Edwardian England*

1901–1914, ed. Simon Nowell-Smith (London: Oxford University Press, 1964), 552.

195. Franz Borkenau, *The Totalitarian Enemy* (London: Faber & Faber, 1940), 122–23, 126–27; Harold J. Laski, *Reflections on the Revolution of Our Time* (New York: Viking Press, 1943), 71.

196. *Times* [of London] *Literary Supplement*, 15 September 1972, 1038.

197. Eugene Lyons, *Assignment in Utopia* (New York: Harcourt Brace, 1937), 243–44.

198. "As I Please," 3 March 1944, in *Collected Essays*, 3:103.

199. John Macmurray, *A Clue to History* (New York: Harper & Bros, 1939), 30. Orwell reviewed this book in February 1939.

200. Review of *The Edge of the Abyss* (Alfred Noyes), 27 February 1944, in *Collected Essays*, 3:100; "As I Please," 3 March 1944, in *Collected Essays*, 3:103.

201. "The Christian Reformers," *Manchester Evening News*, 7 February 1946, 2.

202. "Munika-jataka," in *The Jataka; or, Stories of the Buddha's Former Births*, vol. 1, trans. Robert Chalmers, ed. E. B. Cowell (1895; reprint, London: Luzac & Company, 1956), 75–76.

203. E. R. Chamberlain, *Life in Wartime Britain* (London: B. T. Batsford, 1972), 130–31.

204. Brander attributes Orwell's personal acceptance of poverty to the Eastern element in his personality (*George Orwell*, 16–17), and Woodcock finds in Orwell's novels signs of "some Buddhistic doctrine of the futility of action" (*Crystal Spirit*, 344). In the view of D. B. D. Asker, *Animal Farm* was originally intended to provide the oppressed classes an example of "quietist inactivity" ("The Modern Bestiary: Animal Fiction from Hardy to Orwell," Ph.D. diss., University of British Columbia, 1978, 97).

205. Review of "The Communist International" (Borkenau), 22 September 1938, in *Collected Essays*, 1:351.

—— SELECTED BIBLIOGRAPHY

Primary Sources

Animal Farm. New York: Harcourt, Brace, 1946.

Burmese Days. New York: Harcourt, Brace & World, 1962.

"The Christian Reformers," *Manchester Evening News,* 7 February 1946.

A Clergyman's Daughter. New York: Harcourt, Brace, 1960.

The Collected Essays, Journalism and Letters of George Orwell. 4 vols. Edited by Sonia Orwell and Ian Angus. New York: Harcourt, Brace & World, 1968.

Coming Up for Air. New York: Harcourt, Brace, 1950.

"Countryman's World." *Manchester Evening News,* 23 March 1944, 2.

Down and Out in Paris and London. London: Secker & Warburg, 1960.

"Fascism and Democracy." In *The Betrayal of the Left,* edited by Victor Gollancz, 206–15. London: Victor Gollancz, 1941.

"The Freedom of the Press." *Times Literary Supplement,* 15 September 1972, 1037–39.

Homage to Catalonia. New York: Harcourt, Brace, 1952.

"The Intellectual Revolt (1)." *Manchester Evening News,* 24 January 1946, 2.

Keep the Aspidistra Flying. New York: Harcourt, Brace & World, 1968.

Literary notebook no. 1 [1939/40–1946/47]. Orwell Archive, University College, London.

Literary notebook no. 3 [1949]. Orwell Archive, University College, London.

Nineteen Eighty-Four. New York: Harcourt, Brace & World, 1949.

Orwell: The War Broadcasts. Edited by W. J. West. London: Duckworth/BBC, 1985.

Orwell: The War Commentaries. edited by W. J. West. London: Duckworth/BBC, 1985.

The Road to Wigan Pier. New York: Harcourt Brace Jovanovich, 1958.

Secondary Sources

1. Books

Alldritt, Keith. *The Making of George Orwell: An Essay in Literary History.* New York: St. Martin's Press, 1969. Discusses the virtues and inadequacies of the beast fable used for the purpose of political commentary.

Büthe, Lutz. *Auf den Spuren George Orwells: eine soziale Biographie.* Hamburg: Junius Verlag, 1984. Deals with the contribution of *Animal Farm* to postwar attitudes toward the Soviet Union and technical problems of the allegorical beast fable.

Calder, Jennie. *Chronicles of Conscience: A Study of George Orwell and Arthur Koestler.* London: Secker & Warburg, 1968. The success of the political allegory based on effective, sympathetic use of animals.

Greenblatt, Stephen Jay. *Three Modern Satirists: Waugh, Orwell, and Huxley.* New Haven: Yale University Press, 1965. Notes ironic disparity between light tone of the beast fable and the pessimistic theme.

Hammond, J. R. *A George Orwell Companion: A Guide to the Novels, Documentaries, and Essays.* London: Macmillan, 1982. Deals with *Animal Farm* as satire on totalitarianism of any kind, Orwell's understanding of the animal mind, and the distancing of the Orwellian narrator.

Hoggart, Richard. *Speaking to Each Other.* Vol. 2. New York: Oxford University Press, 1970. In essay "Walking a Tightrope: *Animal Farm,*" a relationship shown between structure and the theme of the corruption of revolutions.

Hollis, Christopher. *A Study of George Orwell: The Man And His Works.* Chicago: Henry Regnery, 1956. Traces Orwell's ideas regarding political power-hunger to such intellectual sources as Karl Marx, Lord Acton, and James Burnham.

Hunter, Lynette. *George Orwell: The Search for a Voice.* Stony Stratford, Milton Keynes, England: Open University Press, 1984. Argues that various literary types and forms used to criticize adequacy of literary conventions in describing and judging political realities.

Kubal, David. *Outside the Whale: George Orwell's Art and Politics.* Notre Dame: University of Notre Dame Press, 1972. Notes the poetic force and clarity of the beast fable and the limitations of allegory.

Lee, Robert A. *Orwell's Fiction.* Notre Dame: University of Notre Dame Press, 1969. By means of the beast fable Orwell was able to examine the failure of revolutions without condemning revolutionary activity in itself.

Meyers, Jeffrey. *A Reader's Guide to George Orwell.* London: Thames & Hudson, 1975. Shows parallels between events of the narrative and twentieth-century military and political events.

Selected Bibliography

Norris, Christopher, ed. *Inside the Myth, Orwell: Views from the Left*. London: Lawrence & Wishart, 1984. Alan Brown's "Examining Orwell: Political and Literary Values in Education" critically examines various assumptions underlying the current teaching of *Animal Farm;* Stephen Sedley's "An Immodest Proposal: *Animal Farm*" argues that a pessimistic view of socialist reforms is inherent to the use of the beast fable form.

Patai, Daphne. *The Orwell Mystique: A Study in Male Ideology*. Amherst: University of Massachusetts Press, 1984. *Animal Farm* a feminist fable linking pigs' exploitation of worker animals with human males' exploitation of females' reproductive nature.

Praesent, Angela. *George Orwell: Krise der Selbstverstaendlichkeit*. Heidelberg: Carl Winter, 1978. Normative statements interfering with the realism of Orwell's earlier fiction effectively presented as political theme of *Animal Farm*.

Reilly, Patrick. *George Orwell: The Age's Adversary*. London: Macmillan, 1986. Points out that satirically reductive devices help to control the frightening historical events by means of comic tone.

Slater, Ian. *Orwell: The Road to Airstrip One*. New York: W. W. Norton, 1985. Discusses the theme of totalitarian leaders' control and abuse of language.

Small, Christopher. *The Road to Miniluv: George Orwell, the State, and God*. London: Victor Gollancz, 1975. Discussion of Orwell's use of animals, as well as his exclusion of certain aspects of animality, to produce a masterpiece.

Smyer, Richard I. *Primal Dream and Primal Crime: Orwell's Development as a Psychological Novelist*. Columbia: University of Missouri Press, 1979. Argues that *Animal Farm* so structured as to keep the animal representatives of the human working class apart from evil world of political violence.

Steinhoff, William. *The Road to 1984*. London: Weidenfeld & Nicolson, 1975. *Animal Farm* as criticism of intellectuals' attraction to revolutionary violence in order to gain dictatorial power.

Woodcock, George. *The Crystal Spirit: A Study of George Orwell*. Boston: Little, Brown, 1966. *Animal Farm* seen as a miniaturization of society in which the dominance of a political caste has replaced that of social class.

Wykes, David. *A Preface to Orwell*. New York: Longman, 1987. Despite its beast fable simplicity, *Animal Farm* exhibits qualities of Shakespearian tragedy.

Zwerdling, Alex. *Orwell and the Left*. New Haven: Yale University Press, 1974. As a work of fantasy, *Animal Farm* functions as a paradigm of revolutionary failure in general.

2. Articles

Cook, Richard. "Rudyard Kipling and George Orwell." *Modern Fiction Studies* 7, no. 2 (1961):125–35. *Animal Farm* as an elaboration on Kipling's story "A Walking Delegate."

Jones, Myrddin. "Orwell, Wells and the Animal Fable." *English* 33, no. 146 (1984):127–36. Points out thematic parallels and differences between *Animal Farm* and *The Island of Doctor Moreau*.

Müller, W. G. "Formen des Alogischen in George Orwells *Animal Farm*." *Literatur in Wissenschaft und Unterricht* 12 (1979):22–36. Discussion of Orwell's use of the absurd, the grotesque, and the paradoxical.

Pinsker, Sanford. "A Note to the Teaching of Orwell's *Animal Farm*." *CEA Critic: Official Journal of the College English Association* 39, no. 2 (1977):18–19. The names Animal Farm and Manor Farm as useful starting points for class discussion.

3. Bibliographies

Bulletin of Bibliography and Magazine Notes: Zoltan G. Zeke and William White, "George Orwell: A Selected Bibliography," 23, no. 5 (1961):110–14; Zoltan G. Zeke and William White, "Orwelliana," 23, no. 6 (1961):140–44; Zoltan G. Zeke and William White, "Orwelliana," 23, no. 7 (1962):166–68; Jennifer McDowell, "George Orwell: Bibliographical Addenda," 23, no. 10 (1963):224–29; Jennifer McDowell, "George Orwell: Bibliographical Addenda," 24, no. 1 (1963):19–24; Jennifer McDowell, "George Orwell: Bibliographical Addenda," 24, no. 2 (1963):36–40; I. R. Willison and Ian Angus, "George Orwell: Bibliographical Addenda," 24, no. 8 (1965):180–87. Lists of Orwell's books, articles, letters, poems, prefaces, editions, and unsigned contributions; also secondary works such as articles, reviews, written portraits, obituaries, films, broadcasts, and theses.

Meyers, Jeffrey, and Meyers, Valerie. *George Orwell: An Annotated Bibliography of Criticism.* New York: Garland Publishing, 1977. A summary of books, articles, and significant reviews in English, French, Italian, German, Dutch, Spanish, Norwegian, and Japanese; newspaper articles, dissertations, and most book reviews are excluded.

Schlueter, Paul. "Trends in Orwell Criticism: 1968–1983." *College Literature* 11, no. 1 (1984):94–112. Books and essays on Orwell divided into biographical works, general studies of his writings subdivided into various critical approaches, and studies of individual works of fiction and nonfiction, excluding individual essays.

INDEX

Abrahams, William. *See* Stansky, Peter
Acton, Lord, 16
Adelphi, 6
allegory, 5, 9, 12–14, 17, 25, 28, 35, 109–14, 118, 122–25, 128, 133
animal story, 25, 126, 127
Asker, D. B. D., 144n204; "Modern Bestiary: Animal Fiction from Hardy to Orwell, The," 144n204
Atkins, John, 14

Bacon, Francis, 63; *New Atlantis,* 63
Baum, Frank, 79; *Wizard of Oz, The,* 79
Belloc, Hilaire, 82, 120, 131; *Servile State, The,* 82, 120, 131
Bernal, J. D., 61, 68
Bible, 124
Blair, Eileen O'Shaughnessy, 30
Blair, Eric Arthur. *See* Orwell, George
Blunden, Edmund, 128
Bolshevism. *See* communism
Bonaparte, Napoleon, 83, 114
Borkenau, Franz, 26, 81, 90, 128, 129; *Totalitarian Enemy, The,* 26, 81, 90, 129; *World Communism: A History of The Communist International,* 26

Brady, Robert, 81, 82; *Spirit and Structure of German Fascism, The,* 81, 82
Brander, Laurence, 18, 144n204
Brown, Alec, 40; *Fate of the Middle Classes, The,* 40
Buddha, 130
Burnham, James, 27, 114, 115; *Machiavellians, Defenders of Freedom,* 27, 114
Büthe, Lutz, 13

Carlyle, Thomas, 99, 100
Caudwell, Christopher, 61, 69
Cervantes, Miguel de, 51; *Don Quixote,* 51
Chaplin, Charles, 116; *Great Dictator, The,* 116
Characters prominent in *Animal Farm:*
  Benjamin, 32, 33, 108, 124
  Boxer, 8, 9, 13, 33, 35, 62, 65, 66, 70, 89, 94–95, 106, 107, 109, 113, 114, 120
  Clover, 8, 13, 32, 63, 64, 65, 88, 131
  Farmer Jones, 8, 9, 31, 36, 38, 39, 40–45, 53, 55, 56, 57, 62, 65, 74, 76, 77, 79, 84, 86, 90, 91, 95, 96, 109, 113, 116, 120, 122, 124

Frederick, 13, 14, 77, 88, 95, 107, 113

Mollie, 13, 45, 55, 57, 64, 91, 124

Moses, 13, 55, 99, 123, 127

Mrs. Jones, 43, 44, 45, 54, 57, 72, 92, 99

Muriel, 32–33

Napoleon, 13, 34, 38, 44, 57, 65, 71, 72, 84, 85, 86, 88, 91, 94, 95, 97, 106, 107, 112, 113, 116, 117, 120, 122, 127, 128, 130, 131, 132

Old Major, 13, 34, 36, 38–39, 45, 52, 55, 64, 72, 74, 84, 85, 88, 94, 109, 116, 121, 122, 123

Snowball, 8, 13, 14, 39, 56, 62, 63, 71, 77, 84, 85, 86, 91, 95, 106, 113, 116, 132

Squealer, 8, 13, 39, 89, 90, 97, 109, 114, 116

Chase, James Hadley, 97, 103

Clark, Kenneth, 70

Cole, G. D. H., 69

Comfort, Alex, 98

Common, Jack, 31, 32

communism, 3, 80, 81; Communist party, 2, 11, 13

Connolly, Cyril, 98, 105; Rock Pool, The, 105

Conrad, Joseph, 127; Secret Agent, The, 127

Crick, Bernard, 20, 30, 31, 61

Cromwell, Oliver, 101, 124

Dali, Salvador, 104–5, 107, 108; Secret Life of Salvador Dali, The, 108

De Basily, Nikolai, 27; Russia Under Soviet Rule: Twenty Years of Bolshevik Experiment, 27

Dickens, Charles, 5, 10, 15, 19, 24, 27–28, 98, 114, 125

Dostoyevsky, Feodor, 5, 126; Crime and Punishment, 126

Drucker, Peter F., 115, 117; Future of Industrial Man, The, 115, 117

Eisenstein, Sergei, 116

Eliot, T. S., 4, 46, 49

Empson, William, 30, 31, 49; Some Versions of Pastoral, 30

England, 1, 2, 3, 4, 5, 23, 24, 25, 26, 30, 31, 50, 51, 56, 58, 59, 65, 80, 93, 105, 112, 118, 119, 133

Fabian Society, 4

fairy tale, 9, 19, 126

fascism, 3, 15, 80, 82, 92, 101, 110

Flaubert, Gustave, 71, 73; "Legend of St. Julien the Hospitaller, The," 71

Foot, Michael, 110; Trial of Mussolini, The, 110

Forster, E. M., 49

Frazer, James G., 54, 128; Golden Bough, The, 54, 128

Frye, Northrop, 17, 18; Anatomy of Criticism, The, 17

Fyvel, T. R., 35

Gay, John, 10, 112; "Gardener and the Hog, The," 112

Germany, 3, 13, 14, 81, 87, 119

Gollancz, Victor, 6, 23, 98

Grahame, Kenneth, 124; Wind in the Willows, The, 124

Greene, Graham, 58

Guedalla, Philip, 9; Missing Muse, The, 9; "Russian Fairy Tale, A," 9

Hammond, J. R., 13

Hardy, Thomas, 31

Henderson, Phillip, 82

Index

Hitler, Adolph, 2, 3, 14, 80, 81, 101, 121, 128; *Mein Kampf*, 80, 121, 128
Hollis, Christopher, 16
Homer, 91
Hopkins, Gerard Manley, 63; "Felix Randall," 63
Horizon, 115
Hornung, E. W., 103; *Raffles*, 103
Huxley, Aldous, 27

Ibsen, Henrik, 97; *Wild Duck, The*, 97
Independent Labor party, 62, 81
India, 2, 74, 105, 130
Inside the Myth; Orwell: Views from the Left, 15
Italy, 3, 80, 82

Joyce, James, 4, 24

Kipling, Rudyard, 19, 37, 45, 59, 60, 74, 75, 124; *Jungle Books, The*, 27, 59, 60, 74, 75; "Walking Delegate, A," 27, 45
Koestler, Arthur, 19, 27, 110, 115, 124; *Spartacus*, 110; "Yogi and the Commissar, The," 115

Labor party, 1, 112
Langland, William, 111; *Piers the Plowman*, 111
Laski, Harold J., 69, 81, 128
Lawrence, D. H., 4, 31, 49
Lehmann, John, 92; *New Writing in Europe*, 92
Lenin, V. I., 13, 62, 85
London, Jack, 27, 49, 103; *Iron Heel, The*, 27, 103; *People of the Abyss, The*, 49
Lyons, Eugene, 27, 129, 131; *Assignment in Utopia*, 27, 131

McGovern, John, 81
Machiavelli, 27, 91, 115

Macmurray, John, 129; *Clue to History, A*, 129
Manchester Evening News, 40
Marx, Karl, 5, 13, 61; Marxism, 5
Meyers, Jeffrey, 13
Milne, A. A., 124; *Pooh* stories, 124
Muggeridge, Malcolm 82, *Thirties, The*, 82
Muir, Edwin, 79
Mumford, Lewis, 110; *Herman Melville*, 110
Mussolini, Benito, 2, 81, 101

Narodniki movement, 119, 120
National Socialism (Nazism), 3, 15, 80, 82, 97, 102
News of the World, 55, 96
Nicholas II, Czar, 13, 41

O'Casey, Sean, 16–17
Orwell, George

WORKS: FICTION
Burmese Days, 28, 33, 40, 41, 45, 46, 47, 48, 50, 57–58, 59–60, 64, 70, 71, 72, 73–74, 76, 78, 79, 83, 84, 90, 93, 97, 98, 100, 101, 103, 129, 130, 132
Clergyman's Daughter, A, 28–29, 33, 34, 42, 46, 47, 50–54, 56, 58, 64, 70, 78, 79, 83, 87, 89, 93, 98, 100, 101, 103, 111, 131, 132
Coming Up for Air, 29, 35, 36, 40, 42, 44, 48, 51, 59, 64, 69, 84, 87, 89, 90, 91, 93, 94, 98, 131
Keep the Aspidistra Flying, 2, 29, 43, 44, 58, 93, 98, 100, 101, 103, 130
Nineteen Eighty-Four, 6, 15, 16, 29, 33–34, 45, 46–47, 64, 78, 129
"Story by Five Authors," 103

WORKS: NONFICTION
"Arthur Koestler," 90, 110
"Art of Donald McGill, The," 41–42
"As I Please," 108
"Benefit of Clergy: Some Notes on Salvador Dali," 104, 107
"Bernard Shaw," 104
"Charles Dickens," 15, 28, 46, 102, 114, 125
Collected Essays, Journalism and Letters, 30
Down and Out in Paris and London, 28, 35, 36, 40, 49, 56, 62, 70, 89, 91, 131
"English People, The," 59, 105
"Freedom of the Press, The," 112, 125, 128
Homage to Catalonia, 29, 47, 48, 71, 72, 73, 78, 89, 90, 110, 111, 124
"Hop-picking," 54
"Lady Windermere's Fan, A Commentary," 104
"Lion and the Unicorn, The," 118
"Looking Back on the Spanish Civil War," 112
"Marrakech," 43, 70
"Politics vs. Literature: An Examination of Gulliver's Travels," 102, 107
Preface to the Ukrainian edition of Animal Farm, 11, 126
"Prophecies of Fascism," 103
"Raffles and Miss Blandish," 103
Road to Wigan Pier, The, 29, 50, 62, 65, 68, 78, 93, 99, 113
"Rudyard Kipling," 37
"Shooting an Elephant," 36, 74, 76
"Wells, Hitler and the World State," 81
"Why I Write," 17, 23, 25–26, 46, 57, 114

pastoral, 19, 25, 46–55, 64, 79, 88–89, 97, 119, 133
Poe, Edgar Allan, 10, 126; "Black Cat, The," 126
Potter, Beatrix, 27, 55, 127; Peter Rabbit tales, 55; Tale of Pigling Bland, 27, 127
Potts, Paul, 31
Pravda, 13

Reade, Winwood, 115; Martyrdom of Man, The, 115
Russell, Bertrand, 62, 77, 81, 82, 94; Power: A New Social Analysis, 77
Russia. See Soviet Union

satire, 5, 9, 16, 17, 18, 19, 20, 25, 97–100, 102–9, 117, 127
Shakespeare, William, 10, 24, 132; As You Like It, 127; Hamlet, 132; King Lear, 132; Macbeth, 43, 78
Sheed, F. J., 67; Communism and Man, 67
Silone, Ignazio, 19, 26, 27, 86, 91, 92, 94, 101, 124; "Fox, The," 92; School for Dictators, The, 26, 86, 91, 98, 101
socialism, 4, 11–12, 14–15, 16, 24, 99, 112
Sommerfield, John, 82
Souvarine, Boris, 26–27, 90, 94; Cauchemar en U.R.S.S., 26–27, 90
Soviet Union, 2, 7, 11, 12, 13, 14, 16, 26, 27, 65, 83, 90, 107, 112, 119; Russian Revolution, 9, 12, 13, 16, 17, 27, 85
Spanish Civil War, 37, 71, 72, 105, 110
Spender, Stephen, 98
Stalin, Josef, 2, 3, 11, 13, 14, 24, 81, 85, 107, 114, 128

Index

Stansky, Peter, 41; *Unknown Orwell, The,* 41
Strachey, John, 61, 68, 69, 93; *Coming Struggle for Power, The,* 61, 68, 93
Swift, Jonathan, 8, 10, 19, 24, 27, 98, 102, 108; *Gulliver's Travels,* 8, 24, 100, 102, 107, 130

Tribune (London), 98
Trollope, Anthony, 98
Trotsky, Leon, 2, 13, 14, 62, 81, 85

Wells, H. G., 4, 19, 27, 61, 63, 68–69, 71, 72, 82, 99, 119, 123, 132; *All Aboard for Ararat,* 69, 72, 99; *Croquet Player, The,* 82, 126; *Island of Doctor Moreau, The,* 27, 68, 78, 87, 132; *Modern Utopia, A,* 61, 69; *Shape of Things to Come, The,* 68, 99; *Outline of History,* 81
Wilde, Oscar, 104
Woodcock, George, 144n204

Zamiatin, Evgeny, 27
Zwerdling, Alex, 15

ABOUT THE AUTHOR

Richard I. Smyer is associate professor of English at the University of Arizona, Tucson, where he teaches courses in political fiction, the short story, British Commonwealth literature, and detective fiction. He received his B.A. and M.A. in German from Southern Methodist University and a Ph.D. in English from Stanford University. In addition to a general study of George Orwell's writings, *Primal Dream and Primal Crime: Orwell's Development as a Psychological Novelist* (Columbia: University of Missouri Press, 1979), he has published articles on V. S. Naipaul, Nadine Gordimer, Michael Anthony, and P. D. James.

1-98 ① ~ 1-99